COLLECTIVE
BIOGRAPHIES
OF SLAVE RESISTANCE HEROES

COLLECTIVE
BIOGRAPHIES
OF SLAVE RESISTANCE HEROES

Lisa A. Crayton

Enslow Publishing
101 W. 23rd Street
Suite 240
New York, NY 10011
USA
enslow.com

Published in 2017 by Enslow Publishing, LLC.
101 W. 23rd Street, Suite 240, New York, NY 10011

Library of Congress Cataloging-in-Publication Data

Names: Crayton, Lisa A., author.
Title: Collective biographies of slave resistance heroes / Lisa A. Crayton.
Description: New York, NY : Enslow Publishing, 2017. | Series: Slavery and slave resistance | Includes bibliographical references and index.
Identifiers: LCCN 2015048566 | ISBN 9780766075559 (library bound)
Subjects: LCSH: Abolitionists--United States--Biography--Juvenile literature. | Antislavery movements--United States--Juvenile literature.
Classification: LCC E449 .C93 2017 | DDC 326/.80922--dc23
LC record available at http://lccn.loc.gov/2015048566

Printed in the United States of America

To Our Readers: We have done our best to make sure all websites in this book were active and appropriate when we went to press. However, the author and the publisher have no control over and assume no liability for the material available on those websites or on any websites they may link to. Any comments or suggestions can be sent by e-mail to customerservice@enslow.com.

Photo Credits: Cover, p. 3 (used throughout the book), 8-9, 16-17, 24-25, 30, 54 , 74-75, 100 Everett Historical/Shutterstock.com; Seregam/Shutterstock.com (chains used throughout the book); Digiselector/Shutterstock.com (series logo); pp. 7, 12-13 , 28, 34, 70, 84, 93, 102-103, 104-105 Library of Congress; p. 19 Library of Congress/Getty Images; pp. 42-43 The Underground Railroad, 1893 (oil on canvas), Webber, Charles T. (1825-1911)/Cincinnati Art Museum, Ohio, USA/Subscription Fund Purchase/Bridgeman Images; p. 44 Wikipedia.org/William Still abolitionist.jpg/public domain; pp. 46-47 Nyttend/Wikimedia Commons/John Parker House from northwest.jpg/public domain; pp. 52-53 Anti-Slavery Society, including Lucretia Mott (b/w photo), American Photographer, (19th century)/Schlesinger Library, Radcliffe Institute, Harvard University/Bridgeman Images; p. 56 Portrait of Elizabeth 'Mumbet' Freeman (c.1742-1829) 1811 (w/c on ivory), Sedgwick, Susan Anne Livingston Ridley (fl.1811)/© Massachusetts Historical Society, Boston, MA, USA/Bridgeman Images; p. 59 From The New York Public Library; pp. 62-63 Universal History Archive/UIG/Getty Images; p. 72 *AC85.Aℓ245.Zy773w,HoughtonLibrary,HarvardUniversity/Wikimedia Commons/ Houghton AC85.Al245.Zy773w - Wheatley, title page.jpg/public domain; p. 79 Public Domain/ BlackPast.org; p. 81 Wikimedia Commons/Freedom's Journal 23 March 1827 vol. 1 no. 3.jpg/public domain; pp. 86-87 The Liberator, first illustrated heading, 1831 (wood engraving), Johnston, David Claypoole (1798-1865) (after)/© Boston Athenaeum, USA/Bridgeman Images; pp. 90-91 Stock Montage/Getty Images; pp. 96-97 MPI/Getty Images; pp. 106-107 © North Wind Picture Archives.

CONTENTS

INTRODUCTION

Pouring rain blanketed the city. It provided the perfect cover for runaway slave Clarissa Davis to escape. For more than two months she had been hiding in a chicken coop with hardly any light or air, waiting for a moment just like this. Soon she would be headed toward the North—and freedom. First, she had to reach the city of Richmond steamship without being caught or arrested.

Earlier that year, in May 1854, Clarissa and her two brothers had run away from their owners in Portsmouth, Virginia. Her brothers made it safely to New Bedford, Massachusetts. Clarissa did not. She hid in the coop to avoid being sent back to her owners. She kept trying to escape. Each time, something stopped her until that exciting day when the city of Richmond steamship arrived in town. Its steward had learned about Clarissa's problem. He sent a message promising to hide Clarissa on the boat so she could escape. But how could Clarissa get there undetected, with so many authorities out looking for fugitive slaves like herself?

Suddenly she had the answer: Rain! If only it would rain so that the police would stay indoors. Clarissa anxiously prayed all day for a change in the weather. After midnight, her prayer was answered; it started raining. Yet, it wasn't enough! That amount of rain would not get police off the streets. But right at 3:00 a.m., when she needed to

Most slaves had no opportunity to escape the shackles of their lives, but some risked everything to flee the plantation or home where they were enslaved.

leave the coop, torrential rain began falling. Dressed in men's clothing as a disguise, Clarissa went out into the early morning downpour. She made it to the boat safely. Once on board, Clarissa hid in a box until she arrived in Philadelphia.

She was helped there by the Philadelphia Vigilance Committee, an antislavery group. Taking their advice, she changed her name to Mary D. Armstead. Desiring to join her brothers and sister in New Bedford, she was duly furnished with her U.G.R.R. and directed thitherward.[1] U.G.R.R. was an abbreviation for the Underground Railroad.

Millions of slaves like Clarissa suffered under the brutal system that forced blacks to work as free, forced labor. Slavery robbed them of human dignity. It deprived them of wages for hours worked. It ignored their need for basic life necessities. Adult slaves, for example, were given just two changes of clothing for the entire year. Worse: Owners brutally whipped slaves or punished them in other equally cruel ways. They killed slaves considered rebellious, especially runaways. Why was slavery so severe? Slaves were viewed as valuable property—not people! As such, they had no rights and could be treated as each owner preferred.

CHEAP, IDENTIFIABLE WORKFORCE

Slavery in America began with a small group of slaves. Kidnapped from their African homeland, they were brought to the colonies. In 1619, Virginia was the

There was much work to be done in the American colonies, and eventually planters realized the most economical way to produce was through slave labor.

first colony to receive slaves when Africans were forcibly brought to Jamestown. Why slavery? White European settlers wanted cheap labor to turn wilderness into farms and towns. They also wanted laborers who could easily be identified. Buying and enslaving black Africans kidnapped from their homes cost less than paying field hands.[2]

Slaves replaced labor once done by other workers, especially white indentured servants.

> White indentured servants, bound to their masters for a certain amount of time, outnumbered black slaves for much of the seventeenth century. The indentured servants sold themselves into service, but only for a period of time, usually enough to pay off the cost their masters had to pay to bring them to America. Toward the end of the century, fewer and fewer indentured migrants came from Europe. Africans, who were in service for life, were used in their place, and by the mid-eighteenth century slavery existed in all thirteen colonies.[3]

How important were slaves? How were they used daily? That depended on where they lived.

> Even when slavery existed in all of the colonies, differences between the North and South became apparent. The Northern economy was based on small farms and on manufacturing. The slave population was comparatively small. The Southern economy was based on large agricultural plantations. Southern slaves had much bigger economic and social roles than their Northern counterparts. Simply put, slavery was much more important in the South, even before the colonies gained independence.[4]

EFFECTIVE RESISTANCE

The colonies won their independence from England in 1776. Yet, slavery remained a booming business. Ironically, it existed even as the Declaration of Independence maintained that "All men are created equal." In 1777, Vermont became the first state to ban slavery. Other states followed its example over the years. Those included Connecticut, Massachusetts, New Hampshire, New Jersey, New York, Pennsylvania, Rhode Island, and the Northwest Territory. Granted, some did not outlaw it altogether.

Even as those areas banned slavery, resistance grew in other ways. Slaves continually ran away hoping to live free in Northern states or in Canada. White abolitionists, free blacks, fugitive slaves, religious leaders, and others dedicated themselves to the resistance cause. These resistance heroes came from a cross section of society. They were political activists. They were writers and journalists. Some used peaceful means, and others advocated change through violence.

Further, they made the Underground Railroad an important weapon in the resistance fight. The "Underground Railroad" should be understood not as a single entity but as an umbrella term for local groups that employed numerous methods to assist fugitives—some public and entirely legal, some flagrant violations of the law.[5]

Even as resistance increased, Northern and Southern states remained divided about owning slaves. The issue spilled over into the legal system. In 1793, the Fugitive Slave Law gave owners the right to retrieve their "property"—slaves—from areas up north. This made it increasingly dangerous for slaves and resistance workers. Despite this, slave resistance heroes continued their important work.

Eventually the issue of slavery split the country. After President Abraham Lincoln was elected president in 1860, seven states left—or

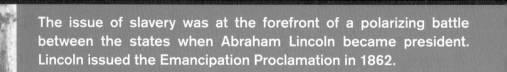

The issue of slavery was at the forefront of a polarizing battle between the states when Abraham Lincoln became president. Lincoln issued the Emancipation Proclamation in 1862.

seceded from—the "Union." President Lincoln refused to accept a divided nation. His refusal made the Confederate states furious. Their discontent led to an attack on Fort Sumter in South Carolina. And with that, the Civil War had begun! It was a bloody, expensive war lasting from 1861 to 1865.

During the war, President Abraham Lincoln issued the Emancipation Proclamation in 1862. Effective January 1863, it basically freed slaves living in states that had seceded from the Union. Slavery finally ended in the entire nation after the Union won the Civil War and once Congress passed the Thirteenth Amendment to the Constitution in December 1865.

All told, slavery existed for almost 150 years in America. Thanks to efforts of slave resistance heroes, ours is the land of the free, and citizens of all colors have the right to live without fear of being enslaved without legal remedy. This book shares some of their stories and the lasting legacy that makes the United States a place where freedom remains a right for all citizens, regardless of race.

CHAPTER 1

ESCAPED SLAVES TURNED SOCIAL ACTIVISTS

Some say heroes are born. Others believe they are made. Either way, the world needs heroes. What is a hero? A basic meaning is a defender, supporter, or champion. Slave resistance heroes defended the idea of a nation free from slavery. They supported liberating slaves. These heroes championed social justice. The term social justice refers to equal rights for every person—in this case, all Americans. The overall goal? They wanted slaves to be equal in every way to white Americans.

It was a radical goal. The only way for it to succeed would be the combined efforts of many people. Those included blacks and whites, free Americans and fugitive slaves, and poor and wealthy people. Many comprised the network commonly known as the Underground Railroad. To help, slave resistance heroes used their influence, money, property, and other resources. Further, they used a mix of bold and secretive actions.

Northern abolitionists served as agents on the Underground Railroad. This clandestine network made arrangements to help slaves escape to safety in northern states and Canada.

Many spent countless hours speaking out against slavery in public forums and in newspapers. Others devoted time to secretly hiding slaves or helping them reach a safe destination closer to freedom. Each hero put his or her life on the line defying proslavery advocates and/or laws that enslaved blacks and called for punishment for those who aided runaways.

Counted among these are fugitive slaves. Once free, they often reached back to help others escape to freedom. Black courage and perseverance, along with the spirited and sympathetic help of whites, brought many men, women, and children out of slavery.[1] Some notable escaped slaves turned social activists include Frederick Douglass, Henry "Box" Brown, Robert Smalls, and Sojourner Truth.

FREDERICK DOUGLASS (1818–1895)

Frederick Douglass accomplished so much in his lifetime that he is by far one of the greatest slave resistance heroes to ever live. He was an abolitionist, newspaper publisher, speaker, author, diplomat, and more. His powerful speaking skills influenced many people to fight for emancipation.

Douglass was born a slave in Tuckahoe, Maryland, in February 1818. His mother was Harriet Bailey, a slave. His father was white. Rumor said that his owner was his father, but that was never confirmed. He was given the name Frederick Augustus Washington Bailey. As most fugitive slaves did, he changed his name after escaping to avoid capture.

Like many slave children, he was taken from his mother as an infant. He did not recall much about her, except a couple of occasions when she visited him late at night. She died when he was seven years old.

For many years, he lived with his grandmother, who was responsible for caring for the children born on the plantation. He had never seen a slave whipped until he began working in his master's house. One of the worst whippings he witnessed involved his Aunt Hester. Their master beat her because she disobeyed his order not to go out that night. Douglass recalled hiding in a closet terrified. "I was so terrified and horror-stricken at the sight, that I . . . dared not venture out till long after the bloody transaction was over. I expected it would be my turn next."[2]

Douglass left that plantation when he was eight, moving to Baltimore to live with the Auld family. His master's wife was kind to him. She taught him to read and write, until her husband stopped her. Douglass knew enough of the basic alphabet to further teach himself, with the help of poor white boys. He traded food for lessons. Douglass was twelve years old at this time, and the idea of being a slave for the rest of his life troubled him. Reading a book by a famous writer and speaker changed his life. It expressed his feelings about emancipation, further fueling his desire to be free.

Douglass moved to another plantation when he was fifteen. Slaves were treated so harshly there that Douglass tried—but failed—to escape in 1836. He was arrested and returned to his former owner, Hugh Auld. His next escape was successful. He made it to New York

Former slave Frederick Douglass became one of the most power-ful figures of the abolitionist movement. His eloquence in relaying his life story convinced many whites that blacks were not inferior.

City in 1838, where he married Ann Murray. They then moved to New Bedford, Massachusetts.

Douglass credited the antislavery publication *The Liberator* with sparking his passion for the resistance movement. The paper was published by William Lloyd Garrison. Douglass noted: "I had not long been a reader of *The Liberator*, before I got a pretty correct idea of the principles, measures and spirit of the anti-slavery reform. I took right hold of the cause."[3]

ANTISLAVERY SPEAKER

Douglass developed his speaking skills as a member of a black debating group. He also delivered sermons at church. His impressive speaking skills attracted attention. In 1842, Douglass was hired by the Anti-Slavery Society to speak against slavery.

During this time he met some people who also would become key slave resistance heroes. These included Harriet Tubman, William Lloyd Garrison, and John Brown. Garrison was an abolitionist who supported "moral suasion." It relied on persuasion to get people involved in the antislavery movement. Douglass embraced that nonviolent approach to resistance.

This is why when John Brown approached him about an idea to attack a military base, Douglass advised him not to do it. Douglass believed it would basically be a suicide mission. He warned Brown that Brown might be killed. Douglass was right. (For more about Tubman, see Chapter 2; see Chapter 4 for more on Garrison and Chapter 5 for more about Brown.)

PASSIONATE IN PRINT

Many people did not believe Douglass was a former slave, because he spoke so well. To prove his story he published his first autobiography in 1845. The *Narrative of the Life of Frederick Douglass* was an important

PLANTATION LIFE

Plantations shaped the growth and history of the South. They were immense farms, producing sugar, rice, cotton, and/or tobacco. Those moneymaking crops were later sold to other countries. Running a successful plantation required lots of work—and money. Forced to work for free, slaves kept operating costs low.

Slavery was work, often very hard work, sustained by force and the threat of humiliation and separation from family and community. Most commonly, it was routinized and mind-numbing, changed only by season of the year or time of day. Slaves did every job thinkable.

Life was horrific. Slaves were beaten to keep them submissive. They were whipped for doing things wrong—or for no reason at all! Many were killed as punishment; others were killed as a warning to others. Owners sold slaves, including children. Hoping to destroy bonds and loyalties, owners separated family members. Is it any wonder slaves tried escaping bondage? Thousands succeeded, but many were not as lucky.

tool for fighting against slavery. The book, however, also was a risky step for a fugitive slave. Douglass avoided the possibility of being captured by going to England. He spent time there speaking out against slavery. He also paid for his freedom thanks to financial help from friends. His second autobiography was published in 1855. In December 1847, Douglass published the first of his newspapers. The *North Star* was published from 1847 to 1851. Thanks to his friends in England, he had a printing press and other items needed to publish it. Douglass followed it up with the *Frederick Douglass' Paper* (1851–1860), the *Douglass' Monthly* (1860–1867), and *New National Era* (1870–1873). He used all of these publications to speak out against slavery. He also began writing and speaking about other issues.

A staunch supporter of women's rights, Douglass spoke at a women's convention in 1848 in Seneca Falls, New York. In 1861, the Civil War began. It was a bloody battle between Southern and Northern states. After the Emancipation of Proclamation freed some slaves, Douglass encouraged black men to enlist in the army. The end of the Civil War also marked the end of slavery. It did not end Douglass's role as an activist.

LASTING LEGACY

Douglass stepped into new roles after the war. In 1874, Douglass became the president of the Freedman's Savings and Trust Company in Washington, DC. It failed shortly after, partly due to the tough economy at the time. In 1889, he accepted an appointment to Haiti. He kept that diplomat role for two years before resigning. He moved back to Washington, DC. He died on February 20, 1895.

Douglass received many accolades during his lifetime. Those continued after he died. The Frederick Douglass Memorial Bridge was built in 1950 in Washington, DC. An extensive renovation project is planned. His home is a historic landmark. Guided tours are available to view it. A commemorative stamp was issued in 1967 bearing his image. Many books for children and adults honor his legacy. They introduce readers to this hero who escaped slavery. Rather than fade in the background, he stood front and center of the resistance movement, loudly proclaiming the liberation message.

HENRY "BOX" BROWN (1815?–1889?)

Henry Brown earned his nickname thanks to the imaginative method he used to escape slavery. Nailed inside a wooden box, he shipped out of Virginia and landed at the offices of the Philadelphia Anti-Slavery Society. Abolitionists freed him from his cramped quarters. Brown stepped out of the box and into history as an example of the Underground Railroad's success, a resistance speaker, and a stage performer.

Brown was born around 1815 on a plantation in Louisa County, Virginia. He and his parents were owned by John Barret. When Barret died in 1830, Brown's family was split up. Slaves were considered property. When a master died, slaves often stayed in the family as other members inherited them. Brown now belonged to Barret's son, William. He moved to Richmond to work for William Barret's tobacco factory. Brown married a slave named Nancy in 1836. She was owned by someone else. The couple had several children. Their owner sold all of them along with Nancy in 1848 to a slaveholder in North Carolina. At the time, she was pregnant. Heartbroken, Brown planned an escape.

SPECIAL DELIVERY

Brown toyed with several ideas but none seemed workable. He kept brainstorming. He prayed for a solution that would be easy for him and his two helpers. One was a free black man. The other was Samuel Smith, a free white slave owner. Suddenly, Brown had an idea to ship himself to freedom! They found the perfect small box. They drilled holes in it for air, big enough for him to breathe yet tiny enough not

Henry "Box" Brown escaped his enslavement by becoming a piece of mail! Brown squeezed into a shipping crate and traveled as cargo to Philadelphia—and freedom.

to notice. The box of "dry goods" was marked "this side up." On March 23, 1849, Brown was on his way.

The small, cramped box was uncomfortable and scary. Tossed about during its travels, it ended upside down for some hours. He recalled, "I felt my eyes swelling as if they would burst from their sockets; and the veins of my temples were dreadfully distended with pressure of blood upon my head."[4] He was only in the box slightly more than twenty-four hours, but it seemed much longer. Eventually, the box arrived at its destination. Brown was free.

Within two months, Brown began sharing his amazing escape story. The written account was released in September 1849. It was published by Charles Stearns and called *Narrative of Henry Box Brown*. The two sold the book while traveling together in Europe. They also spoke against slavery. Brown turned to performing arts, making visual presentations about his escape. The first was "Henry Box Brown's Mirror of Slavery." It opened in 1850. Brown performed in other shows for a couple of years. They were both cheered and criticized. He won an 1852 libel suit in against a newspaper because of the comments about his acts.

Over the next few decades, Brown explored various other artistic endeavors, including magic. The date he died is unknown. There is a written record that he performed in February 1889. It is believed he died sometime after that.

NOT BOXED IN!

Brown's escape was miraculous. That he made it to freedom without dying or being caught is a great feat. In fact, both of the people who helped him escape later tried the same method to help others escape. In an interesting twist, Samuel Smith was caught, arrested, and went to prison. James C. A. Smith, the black man, was arrested. He went to trial but did not have to go to prison.

Brown inspired many with his escape. His traveling shows helped viewers understand slavery and its impact. His story has inspired other performing artists to share it with today's audiences. He is remembered today as a reminder to find creative solutions to today's social issues.

ROBERT SMALLS (1839–1915)

"Strike while the iron is hot" is an expression that encourages people to make rapid decisions in unusual circumstances for favorable results. Robert Smalls is a symbol of how slaves did just that to win their freedom.

Smalls' escape to freedom occurred during the Civil War. Smalls worked on the *Planter*, a Confederate steamship. One night when the captain and crew left the ship, Smalls stole it and turned it over to Union forces. It was a major victory for the now-fugitive slaves and the Union. The *Planter* was the best of all Confederate ships. Smalls' act stunned both sides and made him a hero. A slave stealing a warship? Unbelievable!

SOUTH CAROLINA SLAVE

Smalls was born in 1839 in Beaufort, South Carolina, to Lydia Polite. He was a slave owned by Henry McKee. At twelve, he was "hired out" to employers in Charleston. In this type of setup, owners made money by allowing their slaves to work for other people. Slaves did the hard work. Owners pocketed the wages. Smalls worked different jobs over the years, picking up various skills. One of those was learning to pilot a boat. Although he could not read, Smalls could understand maps and charts. He spent lots of time studying them to make sure he understood where certain things were located. As a slave, he could never hope to hold such a high position as pilot.

Smalls married Hannah Jones in 1856. When his daughter was born, he worked out a deal with his owner to buy his wife's and daughter's freedom. He saved his money. Then his son was born. Smalls had saved about seven hundred dollars of the eight hundred he needed to buy his family's freedom. With an extra child, he worried that his owner would up the price. Saving any more beyond the initial price seemed impossible. The idea of escape took root. His job on the *Planter* offered a perfect opportunity.

THE *PLANTER*

Smalls began working on the steamship before his son was born. He held different jobs. When another slave aboard the ship joked about stealing the boat, Smalls quieted him. The idea stuck, however. The men began planning how and when to steal the *Planter*. They had their chance when the crew left for a short trip onshore. The slaves sent messages for their families to join them on the *Planter*.

Hours before the crew returned, the slaves executed their plan. Disguised as the captain, Smalls sailed past the Confederate guards on duty. He surrendered the boat to the Union. Smalls was considered a national hero. He received a monetary award for his heroic deeds. But, the amount was far less than was usually paid in such circumstances.

After his victory, Smalls helped the Union army by piloting the *Planter* and other steamships. He bravely fought many battles. Ultimately, he became the captain of the *Planter*. He was the first black person to hold that position.

After the Civil War, Smalls became involved in politics. He was a member of the Republican Party. He served terms in the South Carolina House of Representatives and Congress. He is among the blacks with

Robert Smalls seized an opportunity and piloted a Confederate ship full of slaves to the safety of Union lines during the Civil War.

the longest service careers in Congress. Smalls died in 1915. His legacy lives on through the Robert Smalls House in Beaufort, South Carolina. It is a National Historic Landmark open to the public. His name is also on a naval ship, honoring his memory. Finally, occasional programs throughout the country honor his slave resistance contributions.

SOJOURNER TRUTH (1797–1883)

She created a name that highlighted her person and vision as an escaped slave turned social activist. It hinted at her spiritual conviction of having a special assignment—a "calling"—to travel and share the truth about the atrocities of slavery. At six feet tall, she stepped into the name with dignity, poise, and a deep, powerful voice that swayed audience support of antislavery measures. She was Sojourner Truth!

Isabella was her given name, but people called her Belle. She was born in Hurley, New York. The exact date of her birth remains a mystery. She lived on a tobacco farm with her parents and grew up speaking Dutch. She slowly learned to speak English. She was sold several times before John Dumont and his family bought her when she was twelve years old. She later married another slave on the farm that her master had selected for her. She and Thomas had five children.

She escaped one night from the Dumont home with only one of her kids. In 1826, she fled to the home of a Quaker family who was an antislavery supporter. The Van Wageners took her in. But, her master came after her. She refused to go with Dumont. In the end, Isabella was set free thanks to the money the Van Wageners paid for her release. Unfortunately, her son, Peter, was sold to a Dumont relative in Alabama. Bravely, she went to court requesting her son's release. The reason? He was sold after an 1817 New York law went into effect prohibiting sales of slaves to Southern slaves. She won her case. Her son was set free.

After escaping enslavement, Sojourner Truth shared her story. Her inspiring speeches drew large crowds in the abolitionist and suffragette movements.

TONGUE OF FIRE

Religion was important to her. She faithfully attended church. In 1843, her life changed dramatically after a disappointment with one religious group she had affiliated with. The disappointment waned after Belle received what she believed was a special assignment to preach. She also credited God with renaming her Sojourner Truth for her life's new role. Sojourner went on the road sharing spiritual messages, preaching against slavery. She supported antislavery efforts and women's rights. She was a pioneering female public speaker.

Many people came to hear Sojourner. She included her personal story of being a slave in her speeches. She drew large crowds at the free events. One of the most famous was delivered at an 1851 women's convention. Men present at the event had voiced their arguments against women's rights. She countered with statements showing the strength and dignity of women. Further, when her speech was printed in a newspaper it said that Truth had repeatedly used the phrase "Ain't I a woman?"

It is believed that the writer of the magazine article misquoted Truth. Nonetheless, people often attribute those words to her. Certainly, they helped create widespread demand for Truth's attendance at various events. She traveled extensively for about twenty years. She spoke throughout the country, getting to most of her engagements on foot.

INFLUENTIAL AUTHOR

Truth couldn't read or write. She memorized the Bible verses and passages that she used in her messages. Writing an autobiography was not possible. But she could speak it. Her friend Olive Gilbert wrote down Truth's life story as Truth "dictated" it to her. The *Narrative of Sojourner Truth* was published in 1850.

Truth's speeches attracted attention from well-known abolitionists, antislavery backers, and political leaders. She had opportunities to meet people like William Lloyd Garrison and Frederick Douglass. She met with President Lincoln in 1864. She wanted to air her opinions about slavery with the most influential man in the nation. Truth stayed in Washington, DC, for a short time as the Civil War drew to an end. She involved herself in various resistance activities. Her efforts included working with poor blacks.

Truth became ill during the 1870s. She suffered from lingering health problems, some of which were severe. Yet she continually pushed past her pain and discomfort. She died on November 26, 1883, in Battle Creek, Michigan.

AN UNSTOPPABLE SPIRIT

By example, Truth modeled resilience. She made no excuses. She did not let anything stop her. Her unstoppable spirit toppled barriers, paving the way for positive change. She walked thousands of miles over her lifetime simply because she believed she was called as a traveling messenger of truth. Truth's enduring legacy is her ability to inspire new generations of social activists. Her singular message is: You can do it—whatever your "it" is!

CHAPTER 2

SUPPORTERS OF THE UNDERGROUND RAILROAD

People who were committed to helping slaves took matters into their own hands. They created a secret network. It moved fugitive slaves from the South to the North and into Canada. Called the Underground Railroad, it helped thousands of slaves escape. The exact number is unknown. Estimates—guesses, really—suggest somewhere between one thousand and five thousand per year between 1830 and 1860.[1]

ALL ABOARD

The Underground Railroad was neither underground nor, in most cases, a railroad. It

Harriet Tubman shepherded slaves to safety via the Underground Railroad. These activities could have resulted in Tubman's capture and reenslavement.

was, however, secret and sometimes swift. It was perhaps the most clever and unique protest activity against slavery in the United States.[2] Fugitives were hidden in livery stables, attics, storerooms, under feather beds, in secret passages, and in all sorts of out-of-the-way places. They were disguised in various ways.[3]

Most escapes could not have been successful without the support of black communities, free and slave, North and South. Long before there were organized networks to assist fugitives, individual slaves and free blacks offered hiding places and in other ways provided them with assistance in the South. In the North, black men and women whose names are lost to history offered aid to slaves seeking freedom: Hotel employees informed slaves brought to New York City by their owners that they were legally free; stevedores assisted fugitives hidden on ships from Southern ports; anonymous individuals who encountered fugitives on the streets offered them aid.[4] As the Underground Railroad faded into history, the men and women who had devoted themselves to its operations followed divergent paths into the future.[5] However, their work is not forgotten. They include Harriet Tubman, Albro Lyons, Levi Coffin, William Still, and John Parker.

HARRIET TUBMAN (1820?–1913)

Bold. Fearless. Ruthless. These are words attributable to Harriet Tubman. Among Underground Railroad conductors, she is a legend. She slipped in and out of Maryland like a thief in the night, never being caught but always carrying her passengers to safety—and freedom.

One thing was certain: When slaves boarded Conductor Tubman's train, they could not turn back. It was never an option. The ramifications were frightening. Returning slaves could be tortured into revealing Tubman's successful methods. Gun-toting Tubman's attitude? Not on my watch!

EARLY LIFE

Araminta Ross Tubman was born a slave in 1820 or 1821 on a plantation in Dorchester, Maryland. Her parents were Benjamin and Harriet Ross. She was called Minty, later becoming known as Harriet, like her mother. She was often whipped, sometimes severely so, while "hired out" on various jobs.

A freak injury when she was young changed Tubman's health forever. One day, she was struck by a heavy lead weight while in a store. An overseer threw it at another slave. Tubman got in the way, shielding the man. It slammed into Tubman's head, knocking her unconscious.

Tubman nearly died. Unpredictable sleeping spells marked her improving health. (Some suggest these may have been seizures or "black out" episodes.) One moment she was awake, the next asleep. Their duration varied. Years later, the sleeping spells scared many of her "passengers"—but not Tubman. She trusted God to watch over her and her "baggage" while she slept.

Tubman resumed fieldwork. She grew strong and muscular. She also gleaned extensive knowledge of the outdoors, developing skills she used to escape. Later, they also came in handy as she led others to freedom.

Tubman developed a deep faith in God. She could not read or write, but she memorized Bible verses after hearing them. Those provided comfort, encouragement, and inspiration throughout the rest of her life. She also had spiritual dreams and visions. They stilled her anxiety, lifting her faith. She believed God gave her them for guidance and protection.

FINALLY, FREE!

Two of Tubman's sisters were sold to new owners in Alabama. The thought of being sold scared her. She lost sleep worrying about the possibility. One day as an adult she heard rumors that she might be sold. That mobilized her. One fall night in 1849, Tubman escaped! She informed no one of her plans, not even her husband. She had married John Tubman, a free black man, five years before. Tubman hoped to reach Pennsylvania, a free state. She believed God would lead her out of Maryland.

Like other slaves, Tubman believed that the North Star guided slaves to freedom. She followed it. Harriet knew white abolitionists lived close by. She stopped at the house of one, receiving a piece of paper as an introduction to her next "station." It was her first "ticket" for the Underground Railroad. Thanks to the secret network of antislavery supporters, Tubman made it all the way to Pennsylvania. She was finally free. One of the persons Tubman met upon arriving in Philadelphia was William Still. He remembered meeting Tubman. She also became associates with famed abolitionists Frederick Douglass and William Lloyd Garrison.

CONDUCTOR TUBMAN

Tubman lived and worked in Philadelphia. She attended abolitionist meetings. She spoke at some, providing riveting tales of her rescues. Her unique accounts fired up antislavery supporters.

While she enjoyed the freedom she had, Tubman was understandably unhappy. She missed her family. She wanted them to experience the thrill of living free. She made a decision: She would return to Maryland. She would guide them to freedom. It was a gutsy and risky decision. There were no guarantees of success. She had one assurance: God guided her actions.

On that first trip, Tubman hoped to bring her husband back with her. To her dismay, she discovered he had married again. She was heartbroken but committed to her goal. She helped a few family members escape. Her fervent hope was to one day lead all her family to freedom. Eventually, she did. She placed her success squarely on God's shoulders. She humbly admitted she would have failed without divine direction and guidance.

CODED WORDS

Special terms described activities of Underground Railroad workers. These "code words" veiled their activities from owners, catchers, and others who supported slavery. Examples include:

Agent: A worker who planned escape routes.

Conductor: Someone who assisted in transporting slaves to freedom.

Baggage/passenger/package: Code words for a runaway slave.

Ticket: Item given to slaves to make escape easier.

Station: A hiding place. A safe house, barn, or other place where slaves hid out.

Train: Code word for the Underground Railroad.

Conductor Tubman crept back into Maryland numerous times— estimates range from thirteen to nineteen. On her dangerous stealth missions, she succeeded in guiding family and strangers to freedom. Again, estimates vary. Traditionally, it is believed she helped hundreds of slaves ride the freedom train. More recently, historians have lowered the number to about seventy slaves. Either way, the numbers are impressive! Equally impressive are her other activities that helped make her a legend among Underground Railroad supporters.

LASTING IMPRESSIONS

Leading slaves north was a large part of Tubman's slavery resistance efforts. She also spied for the Union army during the Civil War. After the war, she devoted time to women's rights and other endeavors. She died in 1913.

Generations of people have heard and read about her exploits. Tributes include her home's designation as a National Historic Landmark in 1974 and a commemorative postage stamp bearing her image released in 1978. Tubman was a dream come true to the Underground Railroad. She was dubbed the "Moses of her people" due to her heroic exploits.

ALBRO LYONS (DATES UNKNOWN)

Albro Lyons is remembered for his work on the Underground Railroad in New York City. He operated the Colored Seamen's Boarding House there. Lyons was a free black man. He married Mary Marshall. They had four children. He also owned an outfitting store. The family also lived in the boardinghouse. It was a station on the Underground Railroad. The family risked their lives hiding fugitives there.

In July 1863, riots broke out in New York City. They lasted for three days. The protests stemmed from conflict regarding the draft law that made it mandatory for people to enlist in the military. Wealthy white people could pay a price to avoid service. Working-class white people did not have the money to do so. Whites rioted and attacked black citizens. They initially tried and failed to enter the Lyons' boardinghouse. However, hours later they returned. The Lyons family had left before their arrival. The rioting crowd entered the boardinghouse. They destroyed much of the inside. Then, they set one of the rooms on fire. The police arrived so the rioters left. Meanwhile, throughout the city the rioting continued. By the time the Union army came to the rescue, more than one hundred blacks had died.

In 1864, Lyons and his family moved out of New York City. They eventually settled in Providence, Rhode Island. Their daughter Maritcha moved back to New York City many years later. She became famous as an elementary schoolteacher, principal, and political activist. Her accomplishments are part of the family's lasting legacy in the resistance movement.

LEVI COFFIN (1798–1877)

Levi Coffin was one of the busiest conductors of the Underground Railroad. More than three thousand slaves escaped by passing through the depot in his homes. No wonder this white abolitionist became known as the "President of the Underground Railroad."

What inspired Coffin's support of the antislavery movement? Why would he and his wife disobey the law by hiding fugitives? Coffin credits a childhood experience with stimulating his "conversion to Abolitionism."[6]

UNFORGETTABLE CHAINS

Coffin was born on October 28, 1798, in Guilford County, North Carolina. His parents were Prudence and Levi Coffin Sr., who opposed slavery. They had seven children.

North Carolina was a slave state. One day, as his father chopped wood, Coffin saw a peculiar sight. Handcuffed slaves were walking two by two in a long line. They were chained together and led by a whip-carrying man. Perhaps as an object lesson for his son, his father asked the slaves about the chains. One gave a basic explanation of slavery, noting that the chains prevented slaves from escaping and returning to their families. The group walked by.

Immediately, Coffin asked his father many questions about slavery. His father's answers made Coffin sympathetic to the slaves' condition. He later explained, "It made a deep and lasting impression on my mind, and created that horror of the cruelties of slavery which has been the motives of so many actions of my life."[7] Fifteen-year-old Coffin had his first chance to help a slave when he met Stephen. Stephen was born free but was kidnapped while working in Philadelphia. Coffin shared that information with his father. His father shared it with other Quakers. Through a series of events, Stephen was freed. He returned home.

CONDUCTOR COFFIN

Coffin married Catharine White in 1824. The couple moved to Newport, Indiana, in 1826. Over the years, he was a farmer and a banker. He also owned a store that sold merchandise made without slave labor. Coffin poured his money into the slave resistance cause.

Newport was near the border dividing Ohio and Indiana. Coffin quickly learned that it was an active area for antislavery resistance. Slaves needed safe, temporary places to hide. They found a refuge in Coffin's home. He had an upstairs room where slaves could hide—for days or weeks. He helped more than two thousand slaves while living in Newport. Harriet Beecher Stowe, the author of the novel *Uncle Tom's Cabin*, is believed to have based her character Eliza Harris on one of the slaves Coffin assisted.

Coffin used creative methods to transport slaves further to freedom. In one instance, he led them in a fake funeral procession. No one guessed that the mourners were all fugitive slaves. In other antislavery

The Underground Railroad helped an estimated 40,00–100,000 slaves escape to the North. Levi Coffin was considered the network's "president."

efforts, Coffin helped establish a school for blacks. He also traveled to Canada to visit many of the slaves he had aided.

Coffin moved to Cincinnati, Ohio, in 1847. There, continuing his antislavery resistance, Coffin helped more than one thousand slaves escape. He served as an Underground Railroad conductor up to the end of the Civil War. Coffin died on September 16, 1877.

MARK ON HISTORY

Newport, Indiana, is now known as Fountain City. Coffin's former home in Fountain City was named a National Historic Landmark in 1965. Now known as the "Levi Coffin House," it is a museum run by the Levi Coffin Association. The association was founded in 1969.

Coffin's childhood sympathy for slaves turned into a magnificent triumph for blacks—and whites! When Coffin moved to Newport, many whites were afraid to help the free blacks leading much of the resistance effort. Coffin's decision to help changed that. Many of his neighbors actively joined in the fight, providing much needed resources.

Coffin shared his lifelong commitment to antislavery in his autobiography. *Reminiscences of Levi Coffin* was published in 1878. It tells of the fifty years he spent helping fugitive slaves.

As a free man in Philadelphia, William Still worked as an agent for the Underground Railroad. Still is credited with helping future agent Harriet Tubman escape.

WILLIAM L. STILL (1821–1902)

William L. Still helped hundreds of slaves escape to freedom. Later, he wrote *The Underground Railroad: Authentic Narratives and First-Hand Accounts*. In it, he shared the records he kept of his activities. It offered insights into slaves' condition in bondage.

FROM JOB TO CAREER

William Still was born free in 1821 in New Jersey. He moved to Philadelphia in his twenties. There, he quickly taught himself how to read and write. Years later, he met and married Leticia George in 1847. They had four children.

Pennsylvania was a free state. Slaves flocked to it when they escaped the South. Many settled in Philadelphia. Slaves feared the forceful return to the South. The Fugitive Slave Act made that a possibility. That law made it easier for slaves to be caught and returned to their owners. Several antislavery groups helped fugitives. The Pennsylvania Society for the Abolition of Slavery was one.

In 1847, Still began working for the society as a clerk. He was also actively involved in the Underground Railroad. As one of the greatest agents of the Underground Railroad, he helped 649 black men, women, and children escape from slavery.[8] One of the most famous was Harriet Tubman. In 1850, the society restarted its Vigilance Committee. Still served as its chairman.

Still kept records about the slaves he helped. The records included slaves' names and physical appearances and details of how masters treated slaves. He even shared the creative methods slaves used to escape—like Henry "Box" Brown, who had a white abolitionist ship him to Still. In 1872, he published them in his book, *The Underground Railroad: Authentic Narratives and First-Hand Accounts*. The Anti-Slavery Society had asked him to write it.

OTHER WORK

Still traveled to Canada in 1855 to meet many of the slaves who had settled there after escaping Southern states. Another of his activities included an 1859 protest against segregated railroad cars. Thanks to him and others, Pennsylvania passed an 1865 law banning that practice. Still stopped working for the Anti-Slavery Society in 1860. Over the next twenty years, he became involved in various business and civic affairs.

He owned a coal yard, which he started in 1861. His business success led to an invitation to join the Philadelphia Board of Trade. The same year, he helped start a statistical association, which compiled statistics about blacks. He also helped launch one of the first YMCAs for black children in 1880. In 1896, he accepted a position as vice-president of the Pennsylvania Society for the Abolition of Slavery. He worked there five years and served as its president.

Among other activities, he also was a vocal opponent of the American Colonization Society. He did not agree that relocating to Africa was the answer for the problems free blacks faced in America. Still died in Philadelphia on July 14, 1902. His life was a shining example of the importance of the Underground Railroad and its workers.

JOHN PARKER (1827–1900)

Many fugitive slaves fleeing to Ohio became familiar with an unusual business leader. That Underground Railroad agent was John Parker. A free black man,

John Parker provided fugitive slaves with a safe station on the Underground Railroad. Hundreds of slaves passed through the former slave's home in Ripley, Ohio.

John Parker was a respected business owner of a successful company that made and sold more than twenty products. An inventor, Parker had developed a tobacco press that won him an award. Those impressive achievements sparked admiration for one key reason: Parker was a former slave.

Parker was born in Norfolk, Virginia, on February 22, 1827. Like many slaves of the time, his mother was a slave, but his father was a white man. Rumors that his master was his father were never confirmed. As a young child, Parker worked on his owner's plantation. Yet, he did not experience much of the rigors of slavery until he turned eight. That year, Parker was sold to an owner in Richmond.

Back then, many slaves walked everywhere, including long distances to reach their new owners' homes. Parker was no exception. He was chained to an older man and forced to walk from Norfolk to Richmond. After many days, the slaves reached their destination.

In Richmond, Parker was sold again—this time to a new owner, a doctor in Mobile, Alabama. The doctor taught Parker to read and write. Most slave owners warned against educating slaves for two reasons. First, knowledge is power. Reading opened doors to information that the owners did not want slaves to have. It was also believed that if slaves knew too much, they would be discontent. Discontent slaves ran away seeking better lives free from abuse. Second, it proved slaves were not dumb animals. One excuse for slavery was that slaves could not learn. Learning to read and write proved slaves were intelligent human beings.

Parker's new owner did something else that was unusual: He let Parker get a paying job and keep some of the money! Parker worked as an apprentice for a foundry. A foundry is a business that makes metal parts. Parker learned skills useful for the rest of his life. Most of his earnings belonged to his master. However, Parker also kept a small portion. He saved it to buy his freedom. His new owner—a patient of the doctor's—agreed to a price of eighteen hundred dollars. Parker purchased his freedom in 1845. He quickly moved north, working different jobs for five years. Parker married Miranda Boulden, a free black woman, in 1848. They had six children. In 1850, they moved to Ripley, Ohio.

Ripley was an important site along the Underground Railroad. Parker became a conductor. He often traveled across the Ohio River to bring fugitive slaves to safety and freedom. Most of the slaves came in from Kentucky and looked to settle in Northern cities. One of the men he worked with was Rev. John Rankin. Rankin then helped move slaves farther north. Parker recalled this about the men he worked with:

> While the businessmen were not abolitionists, they were antislavery. But the town itself was proslavery as well as the country around it. In fact, the country was so antagonistic to abolitionism at this well, we could only take fugitives out of town and through the country along definite and limited routes.[9]

For these reasons, their work was dangerous. It became increasingly more so once the Fugitive Slave Law went into effect. Park explained, "After the passage . . . , the attitude of the town's people grew even more critical of our group. We had to be more secretive than ever, for it means confiscation of property, a fine, and [a] jail sentence."[10]

Parker kept a journal of the slaves he assisted. By his count, he helped 315 slaves escape. The detailed journal included slaves' names, important dates related to each, and other pertinent information. That information in the wrong hands could cause Parker legal and financial problems. It also would prove harmful to slaves. That is why Parker burnt it, throwing it in the furnace.

Parker started several businesses, including a general store and a couple of foundries, from the 1840s to the middle of the 1850s. As the Civil War approached, Parker also served as recruiter for the 27th Regiment of the US Colored Troops.

Once the war ended and slavery was outlawed, Parker went back to serving as a business leader and foundry owner. Years later, in 1888, Parker received a great honor. His tobacco press received a Bronze Medal from the Centennial Exposition of the Ohio Valley and Central States. Parker died on January 30, 1900.

LASTING LEGACY

The John P. Parker Historical Society keeps Parker's memory alive. Begun in 1996, it has developed different programs. His house— now known as the John P. Parker House—was designated a National Historic Landmark in 1997. It serves as a museum. His legacy is also advanced through the "John P. Parker Award" from the National Underground Railroad Freedom Center.

Parker's autobiography is based on interviews he had with a journalist. Those were edited into a book and released in 1996—almost one hundred years after his death! The title is *His Promised Land: The Autobiography of John Parker, Former Slave and Conductor on the Underground Railroad.*

The book is one resource for learning more about the supporters of the Underground Railroad. Those resistance heroes will long be remembered for their individual and collective contributions leading to slavery's end.

CHAPTER 3

POLITICAL ACTIVISTS

Supporters of the Underground Railroad conducted their work in secret. Political activists felt society needed to see them in action. They believed it was the best way to change laws and make a lasting difference. So they did not want to hide their activities. They did them openly.

Abolitionists of all persuasions considered aid to fugitives a form of practical antislavery action. Indeed "practical" became a favorite description of underground railroad activities . . . "Practical" meant that vigilance committees devoted themselves not simply to dramatic escapes that have come to characterize our image of the

Abolitionists formed local antislavery societies to get the message out to inspire reform. These men and women worked tirelessly to give a voice to those who couldn't speak.

underground railroad, but to day-to-day activities like organizing committees, raising funds, and political and legal action. Many of these activities took place in full public view, not "underground."[1]

At the same time they faced obstacles because of the public nature of their work. In addition to small numbers, abolitionists had to overcome the obstacle, curiously enough, of their own activism. Abolitionists had a loud voice and were sometimes viewed as fanatics. Antislavery agitation was often met with public opposition, and abolitionist literature was even burned.[2]

WOMEN IN ACTION

American women played key roles resisting slavery. They made products to sell at fundraisers. They gave money to newspapers supporting the

Recognizing the similarities in the rights denied to African Americans and women, Lucretia Mott became an important leader in the US suffragette movement.

resistance cause. They supported the Underground Railroad. They called for voting rights for women and blacks. They delivered speeches and sermons. They helped in numerous other ways.

Yet, they could not join resistance groups. Those were headed by men. Many men did not like the idea of serving closely with women. The existing political and social environment stopped them. So, women started their own groups. A society for black women began in 1832 in Salem, Massachusetts. It changed its name to the Salem Female Anti-Slavery Society after two years. It allowed other women to join.

Lucretia Mott was an activist and abolitionist. She was born on January 3, 1793. Mott married her husband, James, in 1811. They were Quakers. Mott became a minister in 1821. She was a gifted speaker. She used her talent to speak up for slaves and women. She also helped launch the Philadelphia Female Anti-Slavery Society in 1833.

The society's influence was so profound that similar societies were organized all along the Northeastern seaboard and throughout the Midwest.[3] Among other activities, the Motts helped fugitive slaves. After the Civil War, she actively supported rights for women and blacks. Mott died in 1880.

Elizabeth Freeman is an example of a woman who also took legal action. She was born a slave around 1742 and was known as Mum Bett. She escaped from her owners and used the legal system to remain free. She later changed her name. She was owned by Colonel John Ashley, a judge in Massachusetts, for decades. One day she left his home and refused to return. Ashley went to court to have his property—Freeman—returned.

Freeman resisted efforts to go back. Instead, she asked a lawyer for help. Freeman wanted him to represent her in court and plead her case for freedom. Surprisingly, Theodore Sedgwick said yes. One of Ashley's male slaves named Brom was also added to the case. The case addressed whether the state's 1780 constitution allowed slavery. Sedgwick argued that it outlawed it. He won the case!

Elizabeth Freeman escaped from her master and then took him to court! Her victory resulted in the abolishment of slavery in Massachusetts.

Freeman and Brom were set free. Ashley also had to pay "damages." Courts make people pay damages when they have hurt—or "damaged"—someone else in any way. Damages in this case equaled thirty shillings. Freeman's case was a victory for all slaves in the state. Massachusetts ended slavery because of her case. Freeman worked for her attorney's family following the court decision. She died in December 1829.

A MOTHER'S LOVE?

Margaret Garner and her family escaped from Kentucky to Ohio in 1856. But they were caught. She did not want her four children to be slaves ever again. Her solution? Kill them. She took the life of her three-year-old daughter before being stopped.

The shocking crime raised questions about Garner and her actions. Was she a murderer or not? The answer and her punishment depended on the definition of slaves. Were they property or people? The crime sparked lots of debate. Abolitionists saw Garner's actions as proof slavery was so cruel slaves would choose death over bondage. Eventually, Garner was charged only with destroying property.

(continued on the next page)

(continued from previous page)

Toni Morrison is a well-known novelist. She has won the Nobel Prize for Literature and other honors. She wrote her novel *Beloved* after reading about Garner. Published in 1987, it won the Pulitzer Prize for fiction in 1988. Morrison also wrote an opera about Garner.

CHARLES L. REASON (1818–1893)

Despite the involvement of some women, it was men who dominated the political arena. This is mainly because of the way women were regarded at the time in America. If education opens doors, then mathematician Charles L. Reason served as a primary gatekeeper. He believed blacks should use education as a means of improving their lives. He helped make that happen. He was a teen educator. He later spent decades devoted to improving access to quality education. Reason also was the first black professor at a predominantly white college. He was a role model for the few black students enrolled there.

Reason's parents were Michiel and Elizabeth Reason. They were from Haiti. They settled in America in 1793. Reason was born in New York City on July 21, 1818. They taught him to value and appreciate education. They also encouraged his talent for math.

DEDICATED EDUCATOR

Reason started teaching in 1832 at age fourteen. He earned twenty-five dollars a year. He saved his money for one purpose—he hired tutors, advancing his own education. Reason had plans for being in the ministry.

CHARLES L. REASON.

Charles Reason devoted his life to education. A school administrator and college professor, he advocated for better educational
opportunities for young African Americans.

However, he did not get into his chosen school because he was black. Reason attended McGrawville College instead.

Reason let go of his desire to be a minister. He chose to be an educator. His career took many turns. In 1847, he helped form a group that was responsible for overseeing New York City schools. He also served as the superintendent at P.S. 2, in 1848.

In 1849, he accepted a position to teach at Free Mission College. He was the first black to ever teach at a mostly white college. Reason taught math, Latin, French, and other subjects. The school later changed its name to New York Central College.

He worked there three years. His next step: Philadelphia, Pennsylvania. He moved there in 1852 for the principal's job at the Institute for Colored Youth. He worked there until 1855. It had a reputation for being one of the best schools for blacks. Reason made it better. He helped raise enrollment. He improved the library's collection of books. He also created opportunities for famous blacks to visit and lecture. The school is now known as Cheyney University of Pennsylvania.

POWERFUL ACTIVIST

Reason's political activities included writing articles and poetry. He also encouraged blacks to go to school. He believed they should have choices. He urged blacks to get manual labor skills needed in different industrial trades. He believed those skills offered a chance for blacks to get better quality jobs. Reason shared his views in 1840 at the New York State Convention of Negroes.

On the flip side, Reason also supported training blacks for careers in other nonmanual careers, like teaching. At the time people said blacks were not good teachers. Reason opened training schools for teachers to change that.

Reason was a founder of the New York Political Improvement Association. It started in 1841. Reason was the executive secretary. The group helped fugitive slaves win the right to jury trials. This meant they could go to court, and hopefully to win the right to remain free. In 1841, Reason fought along with others against the "Sojourner Law." It had allowed slave owners to come to New York for their fugitive slaves. The state abolished it.

Later, in Philadelphia, he also served on the Philadelphia Vigilance Committee.

> [It] assisted destitute fugitives by providing board and room, clothing, medicine, and money. It informed fugitives of their legal rights, gave them legal protection from kidnappers, and frequently prosecuted individuals who attempted to abduct, sell, or violate the legal rights of free blacks. Moreover, it helped runaways set up permanent homes or gave them temporary employment before their departure to Canada. It sent fugitives to the North via other contacts with the Vigilance Committee of New York, with which it maintained a close working relationship.[4]

DUAL IDENTITY

Reason returned to New York City in 1855, serving as administrator of schools. Reason wore his educator and political activist hats throughout the rest of his life in New York. He was involved in different causes. They included segregation in public schools and voting rights for blacks.

Blacks could not attend schools with whites. In 1873, he fought against that practice. Thanks to him and others, blacks had more educational options once New York City outlawed segregated schools. In New York City, Reason also worked with Henry Highland Garnet to fight for voting rights for blacks. Reason died in 1893.

Activist or educator? Reason did not choose one role over the other. Rather, he often connected the two. Because of this, he was an important voice for change in the resistance cause. The fourteen-year-old turned into an adult educator with an unquenchable desire to help better black lives. He was—and is—an inspiration to students and teachers alike.

HENRY HIGHLAND GARNET (1815–1882)

Political activist Henry Highland Garnet is hailed as one of the most important slave resistance heroes of all time. From humble beginnings as a slave he rose to become an active Underground Railroad conductor, a fiery preacher, an organizer of boycotts, and an American diplomat. As a speaker, he delivered passionate speeches. They stirred listeners' hearts. "An Address to the Slaves of the United States" was his most controversial speech. It shocked blacks and whites—abolitionists and proslavery advocates. At the same time, it reinforced Garnet's image as a courageous slave resistance hero.

Henry Highland Garnet believed that attacking slavery from a moral standpoint was ineffective. His controversial call for revolt ignited the abolitionist movement.

PATH TO FREEDOM

Garnet was born on December 23, 1815, in Maryland. His parents, George and Hennie, had eight children. They were owned by William Spencer, who died when Garnet was nine. Garnet's father seized the opportunity to plan his family's escape. The family pretended they wanted to attend their master's funeral. They requested traveling passes. These passes protected slaves traveling away from their plantation. They basically helped catchers tell the difference between fugitive slaves and those on the road with their master's permission.

The lie worked! With the passes, the Garnets left the plantation. They succeeded in escaping to Delaware. Then they boarded the Underground Railroad. The first "station" the family hid in was Quaker Thomas Garrett's home. Garrett was a busy conductor who guided many slaves to freedom. Sadly, Garnet somehow hurt his leg during the journey to freedom. The injury caused permanent damage. It was amputated below the knee in 1840. He used a wooden peg for the rest of his life.

Garnet's family moved north until they reached New York City in 1825. It became their new home. In New York City, Garnet attended the New York African Free School. The all-boy school had been founded by the New York Manumission Society. Garnet studied there for two years, moving on to work on a boat as a cabin boy. Years later, he returned to teach there. Among other things, Garnet also worked as an indentured servant in Long Island when he was a teenager. Indentured servants worked a specified number of years for an employer, often to pay back money obtained for some reason. His boss was Epenetus Smith, a Quaker

KEY INFLUENCES

Education was important to Garnet. After he moved back to New York City, Garnet graduated from the New York African Free School. In high school, he took Greek, Latin, and other subjects. Hungry to learn more, Garnet sought higher education. In New Hampshire, Garnet's studies continued at a local college. A mob attack in 1835 cut his studies short. Residents hated the idea of blacks being educated in their community.

That was enough resistance to compel him to leave that area. He later enrolled in Oneida Theological Institute in upstate New York, attending for three years. Garnet thrived in the new setting. His speaking skills impressed many, earning him accolades as a gifted orator. Garnet graduated and took a job as a teacher in Troy, New York. That career was short-lived.

PULPIT POWER

A religious man, Garnet stepped up his church involvement. He was ordained in 1842 in the Presbyterian Church. He also became the leader of the Liberty Street Presbyterian Church. He was the first pastor. The skills he learned as a speaker years before proved essential. As a religious leader, Garnet relentlessly spoke against slavery. He used his pulpit to share antislavery messages. He also spoke in other venues.

One of his most famous speeches was delivered in 1843 at the National Convention of Colored Citizens in Buffalo, New York. It was a controversial speech. "Address to Slaves of the United States of America" called for active, forceful resistance. Garnet's speech was unlike any he had ever delivered. Many cheered the message. Others opposed it. In it he said:

> Brethren, it is wrong for your lordly oppressors to keep you in slavery, as was it for the man thief to steal our ancestors from the coast of Africa. You should therefore now use the same manner of resistance, as would have been just in our ancestors, . . . Brethren, the time has come when you must act for yourselves . . ."[5]

Garnet added that they "must themselves strike the blow"[6] against bondage, using different means to achieve that goal. It was a call to revolt, making Garnet the first black to ever suggest such action in public. It brought him both positive and negative attention. It forever cemented his place in history as a courageous slave resistance hero.

Leading slave resistance hero Frederick Douglass criticized Garnet. Douglass was a staunch advocate of antislavery. But, he did not believe in violence—the message Garnet's speech seemed to encourage. William Lloyd Garrison, a noted white abolitionist, also criticized Garnet and his speech. That was a big blow for Garnet. Garrison was the founder of the American Anti-Slavery Society and previously supported Garnet, who was a spokesperson on occasion for the society. Ironically, over time, Garrison embraced the idea of political action in addition to his "moral suasion" position that relied on changing viewpoints through persuasion—hence, Garrison's role as a publisher. (For more about Garrison, see Chapter 4.)

Despite the mixed bag of reactions, Garnet's fame as a speaker grew. He spoke at conventions led and attended by abolitionists. His messages influenced many antislavery supporters, black and white.

Passionate about ending slavery, Garnet stepped up participation with the Underground Railroad. He teamed up with Reverend Theodore Wright. The two had met many years ago before. Garnet joined him and others in their courageous work with the New York Committee of Vigilance, all while still leading Liberty Street Presbyterian Church. His political activities took him to England. He also went to Frankfurt, Germany, as a delegate to the 1850 World Peace Congress. That led to an invitation from the United Presbyterian Church of Scotland to serve as a missionary to Jamaica. It was an amazing opportunity for Garnet.

Illness drew Garnet back to New York City. He returned in 1856 and began working as the new pastor of Rev. Wright's Shiloh Presbyterian Church. Wright had died previously in 1848. His reappearance marked the return of his activism in New York City. Garnet voiced his support for allowing blacks to serve in the military. As an influential activist and pastor, he was pivotal in encouraging black men to enlist.

In 1864, Garnet left Shiloh Church for a new job—and city. He became the pastor of Fifteenth Street Presbyterian Church in Washington, DC. It was a powerful position in a powerful city. After the passage of the Thirteenth Amendment, Garnet had another opportunity of a lifetime. President Abraham Lincoln asked him to deliver a sermon to the US House of Representatives. Garnet's powerful words of February 12, 1865, included: "Let slavery die. It has had a long and fair trial. God himself has pleaded against it. The enlightened nations of the earth have condemned it. Its death warrant is signed by God and man. Do not commute its sentence. Give it no respite, but let it be . . . executed."[7]

By the end of his life, Garnet was certain that America was not a land for black people. His solution: blacks return to Africa—or Haiti or Jamaica. In 1881, Garnet was appointed as the American ambassador to Liberia, West Africa. On February 13, 1882, he died in Liberia.

LASTING LEGACY

Among his many accomplishments, Garnet was the president of Avery College in Pittsburgh, Pennsylvania. His push for a return to Africa did not succeed. Yet his legacy of political activism made a huge impact on the antislavery movement. Moreover, it spilled over into the civil rights movements in the 1950s and 1960s. More than one hundred years after Garnet's famous speech calling for blacks to resist oppression violently, the black nationalist and spiritual leader Malcom X would tell his followers that they, too, must secure their social and political freedom "by any means necessary."[8]

CONCLUSION

After the Civil War, political activists supported black Americans in other ways. They fought for rights for blacks. Many also supported women's rights. All of the efforts helped blacks and women gain important rights. Although the end of slavery was indeed a tremendous victory, emancipation brought with it a number of new social questions—for the emancipated slaves, called freedmen, concerns arose about education, economic independence, and political participation. Those most likely to help them voice these concerns were usually former abolitionists.[9]

CHAPTER 4

WRITERS AND
JOURNALISTS

Phillis Wheatley began life in America as a seven-year-old slave but died at thirty-one, a free woman celebrated for her published poetry. In fact, Wheatley was the first black woman to publish a book of poems. Her success made many whites question the belief that Africans were brutes without intelligence, feelings, or other human attributes. Hers was an unlikely success story.

Wheatley was born in Africa in 1753. Slave traders stole her from her homeland when she was seven years old. They brought her to Boston, Massachusetts, on a ship named Phillis—the inspiration for her first name. She was sold to John and Susannah Wheatley. Like other slaves, she took her masters' last name. Wheatley suffered from asthma throughout her life.

Phillis Wheatley learned to read and write from her master's family. She used that skill to pen powerful poems that attracted attention in the United States and abroad.

Her masters initially planned for her to be a household servant. She was bought because the other slaves in the household were getting older. But once she showed unusual skill in learning to speak, read, and write English, her owners did not give her many chores. In an astonishingly short time, she also learned to read literature in Greek and Latin. Her owners also allowed her to study such topics as geography and astronomy. Hers was an amazing education for a slave. Actually, in many ways, she was treated better than most slaves at that time. She never suffered any of the cruel treatment they endured.

Wheatley started writing poems at fourteen. Her owners were surprised, pleased, and supportive of her remarkable skills. They liked to show off her skills. Wheatley wrote about many subjects. She also wrote poems on request, penning them for births, deaths, and other occasions. She soon became famous and attracted people from other colonies who wanted to meet the slave with such talent.

She dreamed of having her poems published. She encountered obstacles in the colonies. Wheatley went to London where *Poems on Various Subjects, Religious and Moral* was published in 1773. It was her first book. Many people had heard about her. She was celebrated for her success and had the opportunity to meet many influential people.

Some, however, did not believe she was the real author of the collection. Her gift of language caused some skepticism, perhaps because of her age and their racism, and to rebut such skeptics, Wheatley's publisher included a letter from Mr. Wheatley, as well as signed testimony from sixteen other notables, including the governor of Massachusetts, Thomas Hutchison, and even John Hancock, to vouch for the authenticity of her writings.[1]

If some critics at the time failed to praise the quality of her poetry, they were more than offset by the number of people who turned to Wheatley's work for inspiration. The political significance stems from the attention she drew to her successful education, and her poems were reissued in the 1830s by abolitionists who were eager to use Wheatley and her work as an example of the human potential of blacks.[2]

POEMS

ON

VARIOUS SUBJECTS,

RELIGIOUS AND MORAL.

BY

PHILLIS WHEATLEY,

NEGRO SERVANT to Mr. JOHN WHEATLEY,
of BOSTON, in NEW ENGLAND.

LONDON:

Printed for A. BELL, Bookseller, Aldgate; and sold by
Messrs. COX and BERRY, King-Street, BOSTON.

MDCCLXXIII.

Phillis Wheatley's poetry was published in 1773. Her poems referenced slavery and Christianity, and also the struggles felt by the American colonists.

Two life-changing events happened to Wheatley in 1778. She was set free after the death of John Wheatley. She also married a free black man named John Peters. They had three children. Two died as infants, and the last child died soon after Wheatley did on December 5, 1784. Several circumstances, including her husband's debt, had plunged Wheatley into poverty. Wheatley's other collection of poems was never published due to lack of financial support.

UNDERSTANDING CENSORSHIP

Shut up! That is the message of censorship. It aims to quiet anyone who opposes a majority opinion. The overall goal is preventing free speech in any form. Targets are often writers, speakers, and publishers. Banning books is a type of censorship.

Proslavery backers wanted the right to own slaves forever. So, they tried to hush antislavery voices. But the truth about slavery was shared by slave resistance heroes in various medias of the day. Their efforts played a key role in helping end slavery in America. .

Frederick Douglass and William Still provided written insight into what was happening at the time. If you haven't read either of their books, ask a librarian for help finding a copy.

Wheatley's work has sparked controversy over the centuries since she died. Some readers felt her poetry celebrated—rather than slammed—slavery. In a lecture, Harvard Professor Henry Louis Gates Jr., acknowledged the controversy about Wheatley, concluding in part: "If Phillis Wheatley stood for anything, it was the creed that culture was, could be, the equal possession of all humanity. It was a lesson she was swift to teach, and that we have been slow to learn. But the learning has begun."[3]

ANTISLAVERY PROSE

"The pen is mightier than the sword" is a quote often used to explain how important literature is to any cause. Its importance to the slave resistance movement cannot be understated.

> [B]y the end of the seventeenth century writers such as Gerret Hendricks and George Keith in Pennsylvania and Samuel Sewell in Massachusetts had already publicly voiced their opposition to slavery, laying the [ground] for hundreds of other writers who would follow in a broadening current that by the 1850s would encompass whole shelves of literature in every genre.[4]

Mob attacking the

An angry mob sets fire to the building housing the newspaper of Elijah Parish Lovejoy. The proslavery rioters killed the abolitionist and destroyed his printing press.

That literature included fiction and nonfiction. The variety of material is staggering. It included novels and short stories, slave narratives, essays, and letters. Writers of the time also penned poetry, speeches, and sermons. Short and long plays also brought the antislavery message center stage to audiences. One marker of the significance of this tradition is the reactions it provoked from slavery's defenders, which often went far beyond words.[5]

Proslavery advocates attacked writers and journalists—and their supporters. Publishers of these resistance works also faced stiff opposition. Attacks on all of them spanned from counterarguments in print, physical attacks, and even imprisonment:

> In 1829, after David Walker published his rousing *Appeal*, calling on fellow African Americans to resist slavery and discrimination, distributors of his book in Charlestown and Charleston and New Orleans were arrested, and the Georgia legislature offered a reward of $10,000 for Walker delivered alive, or $1,000 dead. In 1837, a proslavery mob in Alton, Illinois, killed the antislavery publisher Elijah Lovejoy and destroyed his printing press. A year later, after a speech by the abolitionist Angelina Grimké in Philadelphia, a mob sacked the hall in which she had spoken and started a fire that consumed the building, which also housed the newspaper offices of fellow abolitionist John Greenleaf Whittier, himself the victim of mob threats on the occasions.[6]

The goal was to silence the voices demanding an end to slavery. The tactics did not work. Writers and their publishers fought courageously against such censorship. They continued penning antislavery material. Slave resistance heroes who were also influential writers and journalists include Samuel Cornish and William Lloyd Garrison.

SAMUEL CORNISH (1795–1858)

One of the publishers of the country's first black newspaper, Samuel Cornish played a vital role in publishing news and views of the black

HUMAN TRAFFICKING

Human trafficking is a modern-day version of slavery. Like the slave traders of the sixteenth and seventeenth centuries, human traffickers' only goal is to make money; which they do by kidnapping victims and selling them to other people.

Targets of this crime may be snatched from their homes, wokplaces, or even plucked right off the street. Sometimes, victims answer ads for employment—like open calls for models or performers. When they show up to audition, they are abducted and taken to another location. Sometimes this place is close to home. Other times, they are taken to another country.

Women and children are often the victims of this kind of bondage. Babies can be sold to adults, who sadly believe they have legally adopted a child. Young girls, boys, and women are often forced to be sex slaves. Why don't victims get away? For the same reasons all slaves did not escape centuries ago. Their kidnappers use abuse and various fear tactics to keep them in enslaved. Some victims may not speak the language of their kidnappers.

Human trafficking is a crime in the United States. Many states have increased law enforcement to stop

(continued on the next page)

(continued from previous page)

traffickers and bring them to justice. Charities and awareness groups have been formed to fight this type of slavery and help its victims. If you suspect someone is a victim or perpetrator of this crime, tell a police officer or another trusted adult.

community. His journalism career with the Freedom's Journal propelled him to the forefront of the slave resistance movement. He used his prominent position to be a voice for those who could not speak for themselves against injustice.

In 1795, Cornish was born to free parents in Delaware. He moved to Philadelphia when he was twenty. There, he received training from Presbyterian Church leaders. Four years later, in 1819, he was licensed to preach in Philadelphia. In 1822, he was ordained by New York clergy. Cornish served in his dual role as a member of the clergy and press throughout his life.

CHURCH LIFE

His many religious roles included serving as a missionary to slaves in Maryland and preaching to New York City's poor population. He helped establish New York City's first "Colored" Presbyterian Church. Over the years, he held positions at several other churches.

Cornish expressed his political concerns in his sermons, which drew criticism from white Presbyterians. For example, he vocally opposed the American Colonization Society's push for blacks to move back to Africa or other nations.

Samuel Cornish focused his efforts on gaining respect for African Americans. As a journalist, Cornish believed he had a duty to present an African American point of view.

To Cornish, the colonization movement placed little hopes of blacks gaining whites' respect. Cornish felt otherwise. He used biblical principles to support his arguments and beliefs for blacks obtaining that respect.

JOURNALISM PURSUITS

New York State abolished slavery in 1827. In New York City that year another historical event unfolded. The first issue of *Freedom's Journal* rolled off the presses on March 16. It was established by a group of free blacks. And, it was the first newspaper owned and operated by blacks. Cornish and John B. Russwurm were its editors. The four-page weekly was circulated in a number of states. Its international reach included Europe, Haiti, and Canada. The paper was an important slave resistance tool.

Freedom's Journal provided information and inspiration. It offered relevant local, regional, national, and international content. It gave blacks—slaves and free—a refreshingly relevant viewpoint through pointed editorials that addressed slavery and other hot-button issues of the day. Further, it included news of current events of specific interest to blacks not provided by white papers. Profiles of successful blacks entertained and informed. Birth, death, and marriage announcements marked key happenings in readers' lives. For these and other reasons, *Freedom's Journal* was a vital part of the slave resistance movement.

Cornish worked for *Freedom's Journal* for only a short time. He resigned after completing the six months he promised to fulfill when the paper launched. *Freedom's Journal* folded in 1829. It published more than one hundred issues in its two years of existence. Cornish tried revamping it as *The Rights of All*. But, that new paper was not as successful as hoped. It ceased being published in 1830.

LASTING LEGACY

After Cornish stopped working at *Freedom's Journal*, he worked with the African Free Schools. He was hired as an agent to promote the value

In 1827, Samuel Cornish and John Russwurm teamed up to establish *Freedom's Journal*, the first African American newspaper in the United States.

of education to blacks. That was a short-term position. He left that to return to church leadership. Cornish also continued his journalism pursuits. In 1837, he established another paper, the *Colored American*. He resigned due to financial and other reasons in 1839. The publication closed on December 25, 1841.

In the next fourteen years, Cornish experienced various life challenges. Three of his children died before he did. His wife died in 1844. He became ill in 1855. Three years later he died in Brooklyn, New York. He was sixty-two years old.

RELEVANT WRITERS

Papers developed after the *Freedom's Journal* owe kudos to Cornish for laying the foundation for careers in journalism for blacks. Other early black press included *The North Star*, *The Chicago Defender*, and the *Pittsburgh Courier*. The early black press's collective voice pushed black issues to the forefront of mainstream media.

Courageous staff members diligently wrote, published, photographed, and produced relevant content on a consistent basis. They were not swayed away from their mission despite those who felt the black press was not objective. It was a moot point, anyway! The same charge also applied to their white counterparts. That's one reason the black press was—and is—needed.

Almost three hundred papers existed at the dawn of the civil rights movement. Their circulation declined over time, partly because other publications stepped up news coverage of the black community. As time passed, magazines joined the ranks of the black press, offering other options for readers' thirst for information, inspiration, and entertainment.

Additionally, print and online publications today are possible thanks to Cornish's early contributions to the field. Today's black press and its staff continue to serve a vital role in America. Their online editions meet the changing needs of black readers in a digital world. All are a constant reminder that black lives matter in America—and the world. All exist because of the sure foundation laid by slave resistance heroes who worked as writers and journalists.

WILLIAM LLOYD GARRISON (1805–1879)

William Lloyd Garrison began his career not as an abolitionist but as a journalist and temperance advocate.[7] However, any doubts people had about William Lloyd Garrison's commitment to reform ended when they read the first issue of *The Liberator*. The paper was his platform from which he fought slavery for more than thirty years!

Garrison was born in Newburyport, Massachusetts, on December 10, 1805. Abijah and Frances Maria Garrison were his parents. His father was a sailor who left the family when Garrison was three years old. Garrison's mother was a member of the Baptist faith. The family was poor, and she struggled while raising her three children.

HEART FOR JOURNALISM

As a child he was not well educated. His basic schooling did include some religious training. Garrison had different apprentice jobs as a youth. The one that changed his life was working for a local newspaper. Garrison worked for seven years as an apprentice writer and editor for the *Newburyport Herald*. He started in 1818 when he was thirteen years old. He honed his writing and editing skills. He learned about the publishing business. He found his life's vocation.

Garrison started the *Newburyport Free Press* in 1826. He borrowed money to get it started. The paper became a tool for expressing his political views. It was not well received, folding in less than a year. Garrison stayed in publishing.

He accepted a job at the *National Philanthropist* in Boston in 1827. From there he worked on various newspapers in Vermont and

As editor of *The Liberator*, William Lloyd Garrison had his finger on the pulse of the antislavery movement. Garrison was also a founder of the American Anti-Slavery Society.

in Baltimore, Maryland. His journalism career radically changed after meeting Benjamin Lundy. The abolitionist operated the *Genius of Emancipation*. He hired Garrison as an editor in 1832. It marked the beginning of Garrison's role as a resistance journalist.

Around this time, Garrison pushed further away from views he supported as a member of the American Colonization Society. The society pushed for free blacks to move to Africa. Garrison was a member since he was in his twenties. He began to believe the society did not really want the best for blacks. He left the group.

THE LIBERATOR

In 1831, Garrison launched *The Liberator*. The weekly paper quickly became a primary voice for antislavery reform. The first issue of the paper included Garrison's mission:

> In Park-street Church, on the Fourth of July, 1829, in an address on slavery, I . . . assented to the popular but pernicious [harmful, destructive] doctrine of gradual abolition. I seize this opportunity to make a full and unequivocal [plain] recantation . . . for having uttered a sentiment so full of timidity, injustice and absurdity . . . I am aware that many object to the severity of my language; but is there not a cause for severity? I will be as harsh as truth, and as uncompromising as justice. On this subject, I do not wish to think, or speak, or write, with moderation. I am in earnest—I will not equivocate—I will not excuse—I will not retreat a single inch—AND I WILL BE HEARD.[8]

ANTISLAVERY REFORMER

Garrison helped form the New England Anti-Slavery Society in 1832. He also was the president of the American Anti-Slavery Society, which began in 1833. He associated with leading antislavery resistance heroes. Those included Harriet Tubman and Frederick Douglass.

THE LIBERATOR

IS PUBLISHED WEEKLY AT NO. 11, MERCHANTS' HALL.

WM. LLOYD GARRISON, EDITOR.

TERMS.

☞ Two Dollars per annum, payable in advance.
☞ Agents allowed every sixth copy.
☞ No subscription will be received for a shorter period than six months.
☞ All letters and communications must be POST PAID.

AGENTS.

Charles Whipple, *Newburyport, Mass.*
James E. Ellis, *Providence, R. I.*
Philip A. Bell, *New-York City.*
Joseph Cassey, *Philadelphia, Pa.*
Henry Ogden, *Newark, N. J.*
William Watkins, *Baltimore, Md.*

THE LIBERATOR.

Is not the plea, that emancipation is impracticable, the most impudent hypocrisy and the most glaring absurdity ever propounded for contemplation? Can any suppositious expediency, any dread of political disorder, or any private advantage, justify the prolongation of corruption, the enormity of which is unequalled, or repel the holy claim to its extinction? The system is so entirely corrupt, that it admits of no ...

two committee men and a constable interfered, and would not permit him to take his seat! He was finally driven away, and the pew passed into other hands.

We purpose shortly to visit all our meeting-houses, and ascertain what places are provided for the accommodation of our colored people. A house dedicated to the worship of Almighty God, should be the last place for the exercise of despotic principles.— But here is the extract:

'With deep regret we have observed some articles in the columns of the "Liberator," of Boston, apparently from this city, in which its inhabitants are implicated; and which we believe the editor of that publication will deem very injudicious, as well as unkind, when knowing the truth in the case. So far from wishing to deprive the colored population of an opportunity to worship God, by the co-operation of the friends of religion with that part of the inhabitants, a good and convenient house was erected a few years since; clergymen of different denominations have often officiated, gratuitously, from Sabbath to Sabbath; and when disappointed in the labors of a Minister, lay brethren have attended at their request, and made exertions to promote the prosperity of their congregation; for many years a Sabbath School has been taught, composed entirely of colored children and adults; in addition to this, if we mistake not, at their request the public school money is given them in proportion to the ...

be elevated and improved in ... mous in opposing their instru... exciting the prejudices of the p... unanimous in apologising for th... unanimous in conceding the rig... hold their slaves in a limited ... in denying the expediency of ... the liberated slaves are sent to ... in their hollow pretence for c... evangelize Africa; unanimous ... for the measure—a terror lest t... to avenge their accumulated w... spiracy to send the free peopl... under a benevolent pretence, ... slaves may be held more secu... is a conspiracy based upon ... falsehood, which draws its alir... dices of the people, which is s... which is impotent in its design, ... the slave system, which fascina... which endangers the safety a... country, which no precept of t... which is implacable in its spir... annihilated at a blow.

These are our accusations; ... stantiate them, we are willing ... reproach.

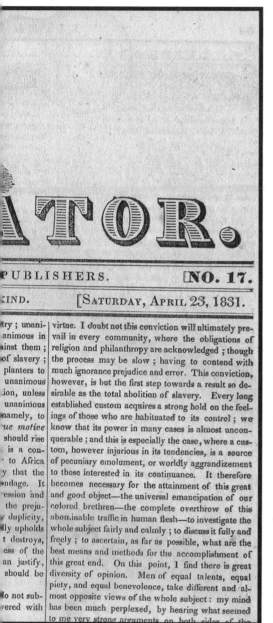

PUBLISHERS.   [NO. 17.

KIND.   [SATURDAY, APRIL 23, 1831.

try ; unani-
animous in
inst them ;
of slavery ;
planters to
unanimous
ion, unless
unanimous
namely, to
ue motive
should rise
is a con-
to Africa
y that the
ndage. It
ession and
the preju-
duplicity,
ly upholds
t destroys,
ess of the
an justify,
should be

o not sub-
ered with

virtue. I doubt not this conviction will ultimately pre-
vail in every community, where the obligations of
religion and philanthropy are acknowledged ; though
the process may be slow ; having to contend with
much ignorance prejudice and error. This conviction,
however, is but the first step towards a result so de-
sirable as the total abolition of slavery. Every long
established custom acquires a strong hold on the feelings of those who are habituated to its control ; we
know that its power in many cases is almost uncon-
querable ; and this is especially the case, where a custom, however injurious in its tendencies, is a source
of pecuniary emolument, or worldly aggrandizement
to those interested in its continuance. It therefore
becomes necessary for the attainment of this great
and good object—the universal emancipation of our
colored brethren—the complete overthrow of this
abominable traffic in human flesh—to investigate the
whole subject fairly and calmly ; to discuss it fully and
freely ; to ascertain, as far as possible, what are the
best means and methods for the accomplishment of
this great end. On this point, I find there is great
diversity of opinion. Men of equal talents, equal
piety, and equal benevolence, take different and almost opposite views of the whole subject : my mind
has been much perplexed, by hearing what seemed
to me very strong arguments on both sides of the

Garrison advocated "moral suasion" rather than direct political action. It supported the idea of attempting to change society through persuasion. Educating people about slavery would change their hearts—or so Garrison believed. His supporters became known as "Garrisonians." They believed slaves should be freed without compensating slave owners. Because slaves were considered property, his opponents felt owners should be given money to offset their loss.

Over time, some members of the American Anti-Slavery Society no longer agreed with Garrison. They formed their own group in 1840. It was called the American and Foreign Anti-Slavery Society.

In addition to publishing *The Liberator*, Garrison delivered speeches on resistance issues. As in print, Garrison did not back down in his messages. Garrison's evolving radicalism on slavery and other issues such as women's rights would draw him into growing controversies over the years, both within the antislavery movement and in the larger sphere of national politics.[9]

CONTINUING LEGACY

Garrison died in New York City on May 24, 1879. He was a pioneering journalist. Thanks to his commitment to the resistance cause, his readers learned about the real issues surrounding slavery. Today, his home is a National Historic Landmark.

CHAPTER 5

ADVOCATING CHANGE THROUGH VIOLENCE

Violence attracts attention. It is in-your-face action that usually cannot be reversed. People get hurt—or die. Businesses may be looted, burned, or destroyed while violent protesters fight in public. When others retaliate, the cycle of violence may continue. This was evident during slavery. It has been witnessed more recently during various social protests across the country.

During slavery—as with today—opinions varied about using violence in advocating change. Slave resistance heroes committing violence cheered their own efforts. They were applauded by slaves, free blacks, and some

89

abolitionists. Yet, they were hurt, killed during violent resistance, or executed for their actions.

What was the reaction of proslavery supporters to violent acts? Basically, proslavery supporters wanted to remove the idea of violence as an option. So, they fought back! They punished participating slaves. In cases of revolts, they used physical force. Slave owners also limited group activities for slaves who had not participated in violent action. It was a way to prevent revolts. If slaves could not freely connect with each other, they might not escape in groups.

Proslavery supporters also responded to abolitionists' efforts. Businesses owned by abolitionists were attacked. They also wrote articles and delivered speeches criticizing violence and attacking abolitionists' reputations.

Slave resistance heroes advocating change through violence helped steer America closer to ending slavery. Heroes in this group include slaves, fugitive slaves, free blacks, and—to many whites' surprise—white abolitionists. Yet, violent acts were frowned upon by abolitionists who preferred peaceful conflict resolution. To them, there was never a reason to pursue violence as an option.

NAT TURNER'S REVOLT

Nat Turner dreamed of rescuing himself and other slaves. He had confirming spiritual

Nat Turner and his companions are illustrated planning their rebellion. Turner led an uprising of slaves that resulted in the death of more than 50 white people.

visions. He knew the messages he received from God were unstoppable. Judgment day—the stage planned for a bloody revolt—was coming. What a day it was!

Turner and his rebels killed more than fifty whites in Southampton County, Virginia. Numerous slaves were killed by whites responding to the crises. Nothing in history compared with "Nat Turner's Rebellion." The revolt struck fear and anger in those who favored slavery. It forced both sides of the slavery debate to question whether Nat Turner was a hero—or not.

By organizing and leading the most successful slave revolt in American history, Turner had drowned in blood the absurd lie that blacks were happy as slaves and would submit forever to the beasts of burden of whites. Now everyone—both blacks and whites—knew that slavery would be stopped. It was only a matter of time.[1]

THE CHILD PROPHET

Nat Turner was born in 1800 in Southampton County. His mother was from Africa. She had been in the United States for only three years when he was born. She was called Nancy by her owner Benjamin Turner. His father was another of Turner's slaves. They were fieldworkers. Turner learned to read as a child. His mas-

The Scenes which the above [...]
dared by his own Slaves.—3[...]

ID MASSACRE IN VIRGINIA.

designed to represent, are—Fig 1, a Mother intreating for the lives of her children.—2. Mr Travis, cruelly murrow, who bravely defended himself until his wife escaped.—4. A comp. of mounted Dragoons in pursuit of the Blacks.

Nat Turner's rebellion was the realization of every slave owner's greatest fear. It also put to rest the myth that African Americans were happy to be slaves.

ter allowed Turner to continue once he heard about the slave's new skills.

Turner's parents believed that he had special marks on his body. Those marks identified him as a prophet. A prophet is a messenger of God. Prophets were handpicked for special tasks. Turner's parents believed that was the case with their son. They felt God would use their son greatly in the world.

Turner's family religious beliefs stemmed from African traditions and Christianity. As a child slave, he learned about African legends from slaves who watched him while his parents worked. His grandmother was a Christian. Soon, Turner was too. He started having spiritual visions about being free. The visions seemed to point to Turner as a deliverer of other slaves.

Turner's father ran away before Turner was nine. Turner later learned the escape was not successful. His father had died. After his death, Turner worked in the fields. It was grueling labor. Turner himself ran away in 1821. In a surprising move, he came back after a month! Other slaves were stunned—and mad. They could not understand why a fugitive slave would ever return to his chains. More so, they could not believe Turner's stance that he deserved any punishment for his escape. The same year, he married a slave named Cherry.

Turner only returned because he felt God wanted him to lead others to freedom. In 1822 Turner was sold to Thomas Moore after his owner died. His wife was sold to a neighboring farmer. Turner launched his preaching ministry in 1825. He was known as a fiery preacher with inspiring dreams and visions. He shared those with other slaves. It fueled desires for freedom.

In 1831, Turner started recruiting for the rebellion he dreamed about. On August 22, Turner and his fellow slaves revolted. They ran from farm to farm killing owners and their families. It was a bloodbath.

Slave owners were furious. They were angry that whites had been murdered. They were mad that their property—slaves—had been destroyed. They were also scared! The revolt proved owners were not as protected as they believed. It also proved that, given the chance, slaves could stage violent protests.

On the other hand, many abolitionists cheered the revolt. They believed it shone the spotlight on the cruelties of slavery. They said that the only way slaves would risk their lives revolting was if slavery were worse than death.

Meanwhile, Nat Turner's revolt inspired slaves. He became a hero, really, a legend, among slaves. They looked up to him as a fearless deliverer, despite failing in his mission. Turner escaped after the revolt. However, he was caught two months later. His trial began on November 5. Expectedly, Turner was found guilty. He was sentenced to death. The hanging took place in Jerusalem, Virginia, on November 11.

OTHER REVOLTS

There were other revolts, including those led by Denmark Vesey and one on the ship named *Amistad.*

> In 1822 Denmark Vesey, himself a free black, was executed after his plot to organize a slave rebellion in South Carolina was uncovered. Further antislavery agitation occurred in 1829 when black abolitionist David Walker issued his *Appeal to the Colored Citizens of the World.* In the *Appeal,* Walker threatened insurrection [an uprising] if slavery was not abolished and if blacks were not granted equaled rights. The South believed Northern antislavery groups were inciting this type of violence and were in effect waging war on the Southern way of life.[2]

The revolt of enslaved West Africans on the Spanish schooner *Amistad* in 1839 had no direct connection with slavery in the South. But it did introduce revolt leader Joseph Cinqué as a black hero, set a precedent for abolitionist cooperation with slave rebels, and led to the organization of AMA (American Missionary Association).[3]

Death of Capt. Ferrer, the Cap

Don Jose Ruiz and Don Pedro Montez, of the Island of Cuba, having p
on board the Amistad, Capt. Ferrer, in order to transport them to Princip
four days, the African captives on board, in order to obtain their freedom,
Captain and crew of the vessel. Capt. Ferrer and the cook of the vessel

The revolt on the slave ship *Amistad* became the basis for a critical
US Supreme Court case, which ruled that the Africans were ille-
gally captured and therefore free to defend themselves.

"The ends justify the means." This cliché basically means that out-
comes are more important than process. Whatever a person has to do
to achieve a goal is OK. A similar cliché is, "by any means necessary."

Is the end result more important? Or should other factors be
weighed? Should some possible solutions be tossed because of their

in of the Amistad, July, 1839.

sed fifty-three slaves at Havana, recently imported from Africa, put them
ther port on the Island of Cuba. After being out from Havana about
return to Africa, armed themselves with cane knives, and rose upon the
illed; two of the crew escaped; Ruiz and Montez were made prisoners.

possibly horrific impact? Abolitionists and proslavery advocates did not
always agree on the answers to those questions as they referred to the
use of violence. They did agree, however, that resistance was the key to
ending slavery.

JOHN BROWN (1800–1859)

John Brown will forever be remembered for his attacking a federal
arsenal in Harpers Ferry, Virginia. It was daring, albeit not wise.

DREAMS AND VISIONS

Harriet Tubman and Nat Turner are among slave resistance heroes who believed they received special messages from God. Visions often referred to dream-like scenes people saw while awake. Dreams usually meant messages received while sleeping.

Some people saw pictures, scenes, or symbols. Others heard voices giving instructions, and other guidance. Sometimes the messages were not clear; they had to be interpreted. Various methods were used. The goal was to clearly understand God's message so that it could be obeyed if action was needed.

The emotional impact of dreams and visions may also lead to an understanding of what they meant. Tubman's visions were peaceful. She believed they indicated safe travels and successful journeys. She was right. Turner's were more colorful and violent. He interpreted them to mean that he would have to resist slavery through violence. He also believed they meant people would die as he carried out God's instruction. Turner was right.

Federal troops were well able to defend themselves and Harpers Ferry. Brown's violent actions forced people to consider why a white abolitionist would take such desperate measures. He is remembered as a hero because those actions further pushed the resistance cause closer to its goal: ending slavery.

LIFE IN THE BACKGROUND

John Brown was born in Torrington, Connecticut, in 1800. His family was religious and opposed slavery. They were devout Christians who saw others as their neighbors and treated them well—including slaves. Brown's family moved to Ohio in 1805. The area they settled in was active in antislavery resistance. His father was an abolitionist with a station on the Underground Railroad. Brown followed his footsteps when he grew up. Years later, he also was an abolitionist and an Underground Railroad worker.

Brown read a Bible verse that changed his life. It was Ecclesiastes 4:1: "Behold the tears of such as were oppressed and they had no comforter, and on the side of their oppressors there was power. But they had no comforter." Brown felt it was a coded message, directing him to help slaves. He wanted to be a comforter, freeing them from their "oppressors"—slave owners. That day, he began making plans on how to save thousands of slaves.

Brown married twice. He had numerous children. He worked various jobs. Over the years, he moved around the country. He lived in Ohio, Pennsylvania, Massachusetts, New York, and Virginia. Brown also lived in North Elba, New York. He moved there in 1849 to help blacks who had received land to farm.

Brown was an abolitionist and an agent of the Underground Railroad. He also helped fugitive slaves in other ways. He gave them some of his land. He also was a founder of an organization designed to keep slaves from being caught by slave catchers.

Abolitionist John Brown assembled a group of men to stage an ill-fated raid on a federal arsenal at Harpers Ferry. Brown's plan was to use the arms to emancipate slaves and to build an army.

"BLEEDING KANSAS"

The Kansas-Nebraska Act of 1854 paved the way for an expansion of slavery. It split the area into two territories, which later became Kansas and Nebraska. It allowed each to decide whether it would or would not allow slaves. This legislation provided that the residents of the two territories—they were not yet states—could make their own decisions on the question of slavery. Especially in Kansas, proslavery and antislavery forces struggled for control of the territorial government, with the antislavery side eventually winning.[4]

When the law passed, people flocked to the areas, hoping their vote would make the difference. Abolitionists and proslavery advocates clashed. Violence rocked Kansas. Brown and his sons traveled to Kansas. They wanted to make sure Kansas did not become a slave state. Brown took an unusual step during the "Bleeding Kansas" riots. He and his sons attacked proslavery residents, killing five. His actions attracted attention from people in the North who believed in violent resistance. In the violence that broke out, Brown's sons were killed. But, their efforts ensured Kansas was a new, free state.

HARPERS FERRY RAID

Brown went back home to New York. But, he had devised a plan to free slaves. He shared it with various abolitionists. One was Harriet Tubman. She met with Brown, agreeing to help him. Brown had a chance to meet the famous abolitionist Frederick Douglass in 1847. He shared his plan with Douglass, revealing how he could make the entire system of slavery collapse. His plan was based on ending the financial benefit of slavery. He was not thinking of violence. Instead, he wanted to spark "liberation raids."

The plan was simple to Brown. He and some friends would free groups of slaves at a time. He would then direct them to the Allegheny Mountains. Healthy slaves would join his new army, helping other slaves escape. Weaker slaves would keep heading to Canada. Brown believed

1, 1861.]   HAR ER'S WEEKLY.

THE BURNING OF THE UNITED STATES ARSENAL AT HARPER'S FERRY, 10 P.M. APRIL 18

As the arsenal at Harper's Ferry burned, US troops transported munitions stored inside to safety. Ten of Brown's men, including two of his sons, were killed in the raid.

SKETCHED BY D. H. STROTHER.]

owners would be ruined if slaves disappeared in groups. He hoped they would lose money. And, he also believed that owners would be afraid. Douglass did not think Brown's idea was a good one. Douglass refused to get involved, as did other abolitionists.

Nonetheless, Brown formed an "army" of twenty-two men. Most were white. His sons were among the seventeen white men rioting. They did not have enough supplies for their plan, so Brown decided to get some. On October 16 through 18, 1859, Brown led an attack on the United States Arsenal at Harpers Ferry, Virginia. Federal troops commanded by Colonel Robert E. Lee put down the assault, killing ten men in the process, two of whom were Brown's sons. Brown himself was captured.[5]

TRIAL AND PUNISHMENT

Brown had to face charges regarding his actions. He was tried and convicted of treason. Before he heard his sentence, he spoke to the court. In his speech, he said:

. . . I deny everything but what I have all along admitted, of a design on my part to free slaves . . . I never did intend murder or treason, or the destruction of property, or to excite or incite the slaves to rebellion . . . I believe to have interfered as I have done, . . . in behalf of His [God's] poor, is

This iithograph depicts the myth of John Brown stopping to kiss a slave child on his way to the scaffold. Brown was hanged for his crimes but lived on as an abolitionist legend.

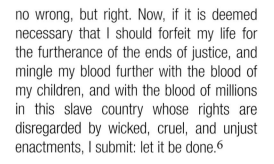

no wrong, but right. Now, if it is deemed necessary that I should forfeit my life for the furtherance of the ends of justice, and mingle my blood further with the blood of my children, and with the blood of millions in this slave country whose rights are disregarded by wicked, cruel, and unjust enactments, I submit: let it be done.[6]

Brown was sentenced to death. In early December, he was hanged. His body was taken back to North Elba, New York, for burial. The place became a shrine for those who opposed slavery.

John Brown's actions, indeed, sparked mixed reactions. Proslavery advocates felt he had betrayed his country. Abolitionists believed he was a hero, willing to sacrifice his life for the cause he proudly supported. His life and story caused tension in the South and North. Not only did the incident compound tension, but it also led to the ever-present question about method and strategy: how to go about attaining emancipation. The John Brown affair reminded many people of the Nat Turner revolt of 1831.[7]

BEGINNING OF THE END

Leading up to the Civil War, abolitionists continued to use the various means of resistance available to them. Heroes emerged in social and political areas, along the Underground Railroad, in press corps, and among violent protesters.

The issuing of the Emancipation Proclamation in 1862 proved how much needed accomplishing.

Slaves in Washington, DC, celebrate the anniversary of the end of slavery there. Slaves in the Confederate states were not freed until the end of the Civil War, and many did not find out until much later.

It only freed slaves in certain states. Soon after, the Union army began recruiting free blacks. Abolitionists joined in the recruitment drive. Many fugitive slaves joined and fought for the Union. Blacks, however, could not serve in white troops.

The Civil War proved challenging for the nation. The economic and human costs toppled expectations. The battled raged for four long years. In the end, the North prevailed. Slavery was abolished in America.

News that the Civil War had ended traveled slowly. In fact, slaves in Texas were unaware that they were now free. They heard the news in May 1865, but the army there did not surrender until federal troops marched in. General Gordon Granger publicly announced the good news on June 19 as he read "General Order No. 3."

The people of Texas are informed that, in accordance with a proclamation from the Executive of the United States, "all slaves are free." This involves an absolute equality of personal rights and rights of property between former masters and slaves, and the connection heretofore existing between them becomes that between employer and hired labor.

> The freedmen are advised to remain quietly at their present homes, and work for wages. They are informed that they will not be allowed to collect at military posts, and that they will not be supported in idleness either there or elsewhere.[8]

June 19 was therefore celebrated as "Freedom Day," also called "Juneteenth." Slaves were known by a new name after the War—freedmen—reflective of their newly found freedom. They needed lots of help getting used to their status. They also needed money, clothing, and other everyday items. Many needed jobs as they did not want to work for former masters. They needed places to live.

What did antislavery resistance heroes do after the Civil War? Some continued to fight for rights for blacks and women. Others did not immediately pursue other activities. William Lloyd Garrison on the closing of *The Liberator* said,

> I shall sound no trumpet and make no parade as to what I shall do for the future. After having gone through with such a struggle as has never been paralleled in duration in the life of any reformer, and for nearly forty years been the target at which all poisonous and deadly missiles have been hurled, and having seen our great national iniquity [sin, i.e., slavery] blotted out . . . I might—it seems to me—be permitted to take a little repose [rest] . . .[9]

The needs were great. Many slave resistance heroes and the organizations they belonged to stepped in to help. Abolitionists also pitched in. The government also created special programs. In the coming years, blacks faced renewed challenges designed by whites to limit their full and complete participation in society with all the related benefits.

In his closing remarks for *The Liberator's* last issue, Garrison noted, ". . . I have neither asked nor wished to be relieved of any burdens or labors connected with the good old cause. I see a mighty work of enlightenment and regeneration yet to be accomplished at the South, and many cruel wrongs done to the freedmen which are yet to be redressed; and I neither counsel others to turn away from the field of conflict, under the delusion that no more needs to be done . . . , nor contemplate such a course in my case."[10]

Garrison was so right. He may not have seen a spiritual vision, but he clearly pictured an America where blacks would face renewed opposition. It was true then. It is true now. Thankfully, new generations of heroes—black and white—are answering the call to fight for equal rights for all Americans.

CONCLUSION

Gone are the days when slavery reigned in the United States. There are no auction blocks showcasing slaves for sale. Cotton and tobacco plantations powered solely by slave labor have long been shuttered. Brutal images of slaves being whipped, maimed, or killed are seen only in historical accounts of the time, not in broad daylight as in the past. The cries of mothers separated from young children have been hushed by antislavery laws.

Indeed, today, blacks are free. America has a reputation as the land of the free—and citizens of all colors have the right to live without fear of ever being enslaved. Legal remedies exist to address modern-day slavery. This is progress. This is the United States of America. And, it is only possible thanks to those who dared escaping and to those who bravely fought against an unjust system. All fugitive slaves faced daunting odds and demonstrated remarkable courage.[1]

Equally courageous are the many individuals who helped slaves in multiple ways. Social and political activists provoked the nation's conscience. Underground Railroad supporters moved slaves into free states and Canada. Writers and publishers used the printed page for antislavery resistance. Advocates of violent resistance led riots.

Each understood that America was in crisis. Millions of people were denied basic human rights. They were killed, maimed, and enslaved for life. Slavery prevailed. Slavery presented two choices—join the cause or ignore the problem. Slave resistance heroes stepped up. They thrust themselves into a historic, ugly battle for equality.

No one made an organized call for heroes. Yet, they started showing up. Men. Women. Children. All desiring change and willing to be part of the solution. No one's role was more important than the other. No gift of service was too small. America needed all of these heroes' participation.

They made no excuses. They could have. Robert Smalls faced immediate death on the seas if his plans backfired. Harriet Tubman suffered from chronic illness. Henry Highland Garnet had a peg leg. Albro Lyons barely escaped an angry mob. William Lloyd Garrison had skills easily employable in less dangerous occupations. John Parker died in the pursuit of freedom. Other slavery resistance heroes likely had similar life challenges.

They pressed forward. Others took the place of fallen heroes. All demanded an end to slavery. Their heroics paid off. Slavery was abolished. It still rears itself in other forms, such as human trafficking. This is why slave resistance heroes must be remembered.

Their stories inspire new generations of heroes. They challenge America to resist influences attempting to divide and conquer its citizens. For that inspiration and challenge, and the accompanying courage they bring, the named and nameless slave resistance heroes are saluted. Long may their legacies live!

TIMELINE

__1619__–African slaves are forcibly brought to the American colonies for the first time.

__1773__–Philis Wheatley publishes her first book, *Poems on Various Subjects, Religious and Moral,* in London.

__1777__–Vermont is the first state to ban slavery.

__1781__–Elizabeth Freeman, an escaped slave, successfully files a lawsuit against her master and wins her freedom. She was the first to do so in Massachusetts.

__1793__–The first Fugitive Slave Law is passed.

__1826__–Sojourner Truth escapes slavery with one of her children. She takes refuge at the home a Quaker family, who pay for her freedom when her master catches up to her.

__1827__–The first issue of *Freedom's Journal*, the nation's first newspaper run by free blacks, is published in New York City on March 16. Samuel Cornish and John B. Russwurm are the editors.

__1831__– On January 1, William Lloyd Garrison launches *The Liberator*, which becomes the primary voice for antislavery reform. Nat Turner leads a revolt of slaves against plantation owners in Southampton County, Virginia, on August 22.

__1832__– A society for black women begins in Salem, MA.

1833–Lucretia Mott helps launch the Philadelphia Female Anti-Slavery Society.

1838–Frederick Douglass successfully escapes slavery and moves to New York City.

1840–Charles L. Reason argues for black education at the New York Convention of Negroes.

1841– Charles L. Reason fights against the "Sojourner Law," which New York State abolishes.

1843–Sojourner Truth begins traveling the country preaching against slavery and in support of women's rights. Henry Garnet delivers his controversial speech, "Address to Slaves of the United States of America."

1845–Frederick Douglass publishes his first autobiography. He moves to England to avoid being recaptured.

1847–1851– Frederick Douglass publishes his first newspaper, the *North Star*. He continues to publish several different newspapers until 1873.

1848–Frederick Douglass speaks in support of women's rights at the Seneca Falls Convention.

1849–Harriet Tubman escapes slavery in Maryland and moves to Philadelphia, where she becomes friends with several abolitionists. Henry "Box" Brown ships himself to freedom.

1850–Henry Brown publishes an account of his escape called *Narrative of Henry Box Brown*. Sojourner Truth publishes her autobiography. Harriet Tubman begins helping slaves escape to freedom as a "conductor" on the Underground Railroad.

1851–Sojourner Truth gives her most famous speech at a women's convention.

1854–The Kansas-Nebraska Act of 1854 is passed, leading to violent conflicts in the territories.

1860–Abraham Lincoln is elected President of the United States of America.

1861– The Civil War begins.

1862–President Lincoln issues the Emancipation Proclamation.

1863–Riots break out in New York City targeting free black citizens.

1865–At the request of President Lincoln, Henry Garnet delivers a sermon to the US House of Representatives on February 12. On May 9 the Civil War ends. On June 19, slaves in Texas are officially informed that they are free. The day is known as "Freedom Day." The Thirteenth Amendment to the Constitution is adopted in December, ending slavery in the United States.

1872–William L. Still publishes *The Underground Railroad: Authentic Narratives and First-Hand Accounts*.

CHAPTER NOTES

INTRODUCTION

1. George Hendrick and Willene Hendrick, eds. *Fleeing for Freedom: Stories of the Underground Railroad as Told by Levi Coffin and William Still* (Chicago, IL: Ivan R. Dee, 2004), p. 102.
2. Mary Kay Carson, *Which Way to Freedom? And Other Questions About . . . The Underground Railroad* (New York: Sterling Publishing, 2014), p. 4.
3. Jodie Zdrok-Ptaszek, *The Antislavery Movement* (San Diego, CA: Greenhaven Press, 2002), p. 12.
4. Ibid., p. 12–13.
5. Eric Foner, *Gateway to Freedom: The Hidden History of the Underground Railroad* (New York: W.W. Norton & Company, 2015), p. 15.

CHAPTER 1. ESCAPED SLAVES TURNED SOCIAL ACTIVISTS

1. Charles L. Blockson, *The Underground Railroad: First-Person Narratives of Escapes to Freedom in the North* (New York: Prentice Hall Press, 1987), p. 4.
2. Frederick Douglass, *Narrative of the Life of Frederick Douglass* (New York: Dover Publications, Inc., 1995), p. 39.
3. Ibid., p. 69.
4. Devon W. Carbado and Donald Weise, eds. *The Long Walk to Freedom: Runaway Slave Narratives* (Boston: Beacon Press, 2012), p. 198.

CHAPTER 2. SUPPORTERS OF THE UNDERGROUND RAILROAD

1. Eric Foner, Gateway to Freedom: *The Hidden History of the Underground Railroad* (New York: W.W. Norton & Company, 2015), p. 4.

2. James Haskins and Kathleen Benson, *Following Freedom's Star: The Story of the Underground Railroad* (New York: Marshall Cavendish, 2002), p. 11.

3. Charles L. Blockson, *The Underground Railroad: First-Person Narratives of Escapes to Freedom in the North* (New York: Prentice Hall Press, 1987), p. 2–3.

4. Foner, p. 18.

5. Foner, p. 225.

6. George Hendrick and Willene Hendrick, eds. *Fleeing for Freedom: Stories of the Underground Railroad as Told by Levi Coffin and William Still* (Chicago: Ivan R. Dee, 2004), p. 29.

7. Ibid.

8. Richard L. Green, pub. & ed. *A Gift of Heritage: Historic Back Abolitionists* (Chicago: Empak Enterprises, Inc., 1991), p. 22.

9. John Parker, *His Promised Land: The Autobiography of John P. Parker, Former Slave and Conductor on the Underground Railroad* (New York: W.W. Norton & Co., 1996), p. 99.

10. Ibid.

CHAPTER 3. POLITICAL ACTIVISTS

1. Eric Foner, Gateway to Freedom: *The Hidden History of the Underground Railroad* (Minneapolis: HighBridge Audio: Holland, OH: Repackaged by Midwest Tape, 2015).

2. Jodie Zdrok-Ptaszek, *The Antislavery Movement* (San Diego, CA: Greenhaven Press, 2002), p. 19.

3. Charles L. Blockson, *The Underground Railroad: First-Person Narratives of Escapes to Freedom in the North* (New York: Prentice Hall Press, 1987), p. 235.

4. Ibid., p. 234.

5. James G. Basker, ed. *American Antislavery Writings: Colonial Beginnings to Emancipation* (New York: Literary Classics of the United States, 2012), p. 447–448.

6. Ibid., p. 448.

7. Ibid., p. 878.

8. Kimberly Hayes Taylor, *Black Abolitionists and Freedom Fighters* (Minneapolis: Oliver Press, 1996), p. 69.

9. Zdrok-Ptaszek, p. 22–23.

CHAPTER 4. WRITERS AND JOURNALISTS

1. John Edgar Wideman, ed. *My Soul Has Grown Deep: Classics of Early African-American Literature* (New York: Ballantine Publishing Group, 2001), p. 55.

2. Ibid., p. 57.

3. National Endowment for the Humanities, 2002 Jefferson Lecturer Henry Louis Gates, Jr. Lecture, "Mister Jefferson and The Trials of Phillis Wheatley," http://www.neh.gov/about/awards/jefferson-lecture/henry-louis-gates-jr-lecture (accessed Nov. 29, 2015).

4. James G. Basker, ed. *American Antislavery Writings: Colonial Beginnings to Emancipation* (New York: Literary Classics of the United States, 2012), p. xxvii–xxviii.

5. Ibid.

6. Ibid.

7. Jodie Zdrok-Ptaszek, *The Antislavery Movement* (San Diego: Greenhaven Press, 2002), p. 58.

8. Basker, p. 268.

9. Ibid., p. 267.

CHAPTER 5. ADVOCATING CHANGE THROUGH VIOLENCE

1. Terry Bisson, Nat Turner: *Slave Revolt Leader* (Philadelphia: Chelsea House Publishers, 2005), p. 4.

2. Jodie Zdrok-Ptaszek, *The Antislavery Movement* (San Diego: Greenhaven Press, 2002), p. 15–16.

3. Ibid., p. 108.

4. James Haskins, *Following Freedom's Star: The Story of the Underground Railroad* (New York: Benchmark Books, 2002), p. 85.

5. Ibid., p. 91.

6. James G. Basker, ed. *American Antislavery Writings: Colonial Beginnings to Emancipation* (New York: Literary Classics of the United States, 2012), p. 792, 793.

7. Zdrok-Ptaszek, p. 21.

8. *New York Times,* "From Texas: Important Orders by General Granger, Surrender of Senator Johnson of Arkansas Scattering of Rebel Officials," July 7, 1865, http://www.nytimes.com/1865/07/07/news /texas-important-orders-general-granger-surrender-senator-johnson-arkansas.html (accessed Dec. 1, 2015).

9. Zdrok-Ptaszek, p. 153.

10. Ibid.

CONCLUSION

1. Eric Foner, *Gateway to Freedom: The Hidden History of the Underground Railroad* (Minneapolis: HighBridge Audio: Holland, OH: Repackaged by Midwest Tape, 2015).

GLOSSARY

abolitionist—A person who opposed slavery; person committed to ending slavery.

activist—A person dedicated to helping others through social change.

amendment—An addition to a law or legal document that permanently changes it.

boardinghouse—An apartment-like place where people rented rooms.

bondage—The state of being bonded, often used to describe slavery.

censorship—Efforts to prevent or stop the writing, publication, or distribution of material.

civil rights—Give all people rights to be treated the same—equal—without discrimination while protecting freedoms granted by law.

Civil War—The war between Southern and Northern states that was mainly caused by disagreements over slavery.

colonies—A group of people who settle in another place.

conductor—An abolitionist who served as a guide, helping people to travel the Underground Railroad.

depot—A safe house for hiding slaves.

diplomat—A citizen of one country appointed to represent his or her nation while living in a foreign country.

emancipation—The term used to describe the permanent end of slavery and freedom of slaves.

Emancipation Proclamation—The executive order on September 22, 1862, by President Abraham Lincoln. It made slavery illegal in certain states effective January 1, 1863.

freedman—Former slave who is now free.

master—A word for a person who owned slaves.

moral suasion—An attempt to change behavior by appealing to morality.

Northwest Territory—This northern part of the country would later become the five states of Illinois, Indiana, Michigan, Ohio, and Wisconsin.

overseer—A plantation employee who supervises field slaves. They were often cruel and abusive.

plantation—A large farm producing rice, tobacco, and sugar and other crops by slave labor.

Quakers—A devout religious group; many of the members opposed slavery and actively participated in antislavery efforts.

ratify—Make something valid by giving official approval.

servitude—Slavery or other condition in which one person worked for another.

slave narratives—Written, personal accounts of a slave's life.

stationmaster—A person who provided a stopover or hiding place on the Underground Railroad.

stevedore—A dock worker whose job involved unloading and loading boats.

13th Amendment—This amendment to the US Constitution in 1865 made slavery illegal.

Underground Railroad—A collaboration of people who secretly worked to help slaves reach freedom in northern US states and Canada.

FURTHER READING

BOOKS

Adler, David A. *Harriet Tubman and the Underground Railroad*. New York: Holiday House, 2013.

Altman, Linda Jacobs. *The Story of Slavery and Abolition in United States History*. Berkeley Heights, NJ: Enslow Publishers, Inc., 2015.

Basker, James G., ed. *American Antislavery Writings*. New York: Literary Classics of the United States, 2012.

Carbado, Devon W. and Donald Weise, Eds. *The Long Walk to Freedom: Runaway Slave Narratives*. Boston, MA: Beacon Press, 2012.

Carson, Mary Kay. *Which Way to Freedom: and Other Questions About . . . The Underground Railroad*. New York: Sterling Publishing, 2014.

Douglass, Frederick. *Narrative of the Life of Frederick Douglass*. New York: Dover Publications, Inc., 1995.

Gill, Joel Christian. *Strange Fruit. Uncelebrated Narratives from Black History*. Vol. 1. Golden, CO: Fulcrum Publishing, 2014.

Parker, John. *His Promised Land: The Autobiography of John P. Parker, Former Slave and Conductor on the Underground Railroad*. New York: W.W. Norton & Co., 1996.

Schraff, Anne E. *The Life of Frederick Douglass: Speaking Out Against Slavery*. Berkeley Heights, NJ: Enslow Publishers, Inc., 2015.

Turner, Ann. *My Name Is Truth: The Life of Sojourner Truth*. New York: HarperCollins, 2015.

WEBSITES

Aboard the Underground Railroad: A National Register of Historic Places Travel Itinerary

www.nps.gov/nr/travel/underground/

The National Park Service website of "America's official list of places important in our history and worthy of preservation." Includes a map of common escape routes.

Documenting the American South

docsouth.unc.edu/

Sixteen collections of materials related to black history, including slave narratives, books, interviews, and other resources.

Slavery and the Making of America

www.pbs.org/wnet/slavery/index.html

PBS website offering various resources about slaves' experiences and American slavery.

INDEX